Oracle Demystified: A Practical Guide for Beginners

Table of contents:

1. **Introduction to Oracle Database**
    - Overview of Oracle Database
    - The Importance of Oracle in the Industry
2. **Setting Up Your Oracle Environment**
    - Installation of Oracle Database
    - Configuration Basics
    - Connecting to the Database
3. **Understanding Oracle Architecture**
    - Key Components and Structure
    - Oracle Instance vs. Database
4. **Basic SQL Queries**
    - Introduction to SQL
    - SELECT, INSERT, UPDATE, DELETE Commands
5. **Database Objects and Structures**
    - Tables, Views, and Indexes
    - Schemas and Users
6. **Data Types and Constraints**
    - Common Data Types
    - Implementing Constraints (Primary Key, Foreign Key, etc.)
7. **PL/SQL Basics**
    - Introduction to PL/SQL

- Writing and Executing PL/SQL Blocks
8. **Procedures and Functions**
    - Creating Stored Procedures
    - Building Functions for Reusable Code
9. **Triggers and Exception Handling**
    - Understanding Triggers
    - Exception Handling in PL/SQL
10. **Transactions and Concurrency Control**
    - Concepts of Transactions
    - Managing Transactions and Isolation Levels
11. **Data Management and Security**
    - Backup and Recovery Techniques
    - User Management and Security Best Practices
12. **Performance Tuning Basics**
    - Understanding Query Performance
    - Basic Tuning Techniques
13. **Working with Oracle Tools**
    - Oracle SQL*Plus
    - Oracle SQL Developer and Other GUI Tools
14. **Data Modeling and Design**
    - Entity-Relationship Models
    - Normalization and Denormalization
15. **Advanced SQL Queries**
    - Joins, Subqueries, and Set Operations
    - Analytical Functions
16. **Understanding and Using Views**
    - Creating and Managing Views

- Materialized Views
17. **Introduction to Oracle RAC**
    - Concepts of Real Application Clusters (RAC)
    - Benefits and Basic Configuration
18. **Data Warehousing with Oracle**
    - Basics of Data Warehousing
    - ETL Processes and Oracle Data Warehouse
19. **Oracle Cloud Services**
    - Overview of Oracle Cloud Offerings
    - Migrating to Oracle Cloud
20. **Best Practices and Troubleshooting**
    - Common Pitfalls and How to Avoid Them
    - Troubleshooting Techniques and Tools

Feel free to adjust or expand any chapters based on the specific focus you want to have!

Chapter 1: Introduction to Oracle Database

1.1 Overview of Oracle Database

Oracle Database is one of the most widely used and comprehensive relational database management systems (RDBMS) in the world. Developed by Oracle Corporation, it is renowned for its scalability, reliability, and robust performance. Whether you're managing small applications or large enterprise systems, Oracle Database provides the tools and features needed to handle various data management tasks effectively.

Oracle Database supports a broad range of functionalities, including data storage, data retrieval, and data manipulation. It is designed to manage large amounts of data efficiently, making it a popular choice among businesses of all sizes. The database system is also known for its advanced security features, ensuring that your data remains safe and accessible only to authorized users.

1.2 The Importance of Oracle in the Industry

In the modern world, data is a critical asset for organizations. Oracle Database plays a crucial role in enabling businesses to harness the power of their data. Here's why Oracle Database is significant:

- **Scalability**: Oracle Database can scale from small applications to large-scale enterprise systems with ease. Its architecture is designed to handle vast amounts of data and concurrent users without compromising performance.
- **Reliability**: Oracle Database is known for its high availability and reliability. Features like automatic backup, recovery, and fault tolerance ensure that your data is always accessible and protected.
- **Security**: With built-in security features such as encryption, user authentication, and access control, Oracle Database helps organizations protect their data from unauthorized access and breaches.
- **Performance**: Oracle Database provides advanced performance optimization tools and techniques, ensuring that queries and transactions are executed efficiently.
- **Flexibility**: It supports a wide range of programming languages, including SQL and PL/SQL, allowing developers to build diverse applications tailored to their needs.

1.3 Key Components of Oracle Database

To understand how Oracle Database works, it's essential to be familiar with its key components:

- **Oracle Instance**: This is a combination of the Oracle background processes and memory structures that manage the database. The instance includes the System Global Area (SGA) and the background processes like the Database Writer (DBWn) and Log Writer (LGWR).
- **Oracle Database**: The database itself consists of physical files that store the data, including data files, control files, and redo log files. These files collectively hold the actual data and metadata.
- **Data Files**: These files store the actual user data and are the primary storage for the database.
- **Control Files**: These files keep track of the database's structure and state. They are crucial for database recovery and consistency.
- **Redo Log Files**: These files record all changes made to the database, ensuring that transactions can be recovered in case of a failure.
- **Tablespaces**: A tablespace is a logical storage unit within a database that groups related data files together. It helps in managing and organizing the data efficiently.

1.4 Basic Terminology

Familiarizing yourself with some basic terms will help you understand Oracle Database better:

- **Schema**: A schema is a collection of database objects, such as tables and views, that belong to a specific user. Each user in Oracle Database has a schema with the same name as their username.
- **Table**: A table is a fundamental database object that stores data in rows and columns. Each row represents a record, and each column represents a data attribute.
- **View**: A view is a virtual table that provides a specific representation of data from one or more tables. It helps in simplifying complex queries and providing data security.
- **Index**: An index is an optional database object that improves the speed of data retrieval operations by creating a data structure that allows faster searches.

1.5 Oracle Database Editions

Oracle offers various editions of its database software to cater to different needs:

- **Oracle Database Express Edition (XE)**: A free, lightweight edition suitable for small applications and learning purposes.
- **Oracle Database Standard Edition**: Designed for small to medium-sized businesses, it includes core features for data management.

- **Oracle Database Enterprise Edition**: The most comprehensive edition, offering advanced features for large enterprises, including high availability, security, and performance optimization tools.
- **Oracle Database Cloud Services**: Cloud-based editions provide the flexibility of cloud computing along with Oracle's robust database features.

1.6 Getting Started with Oracle Database

To begin using Oracle Database, you will need to:

1. **Download and Install**: Obtain the Oracle Database software from the Oracle website and follow the installation instructions for your operating system.
2. **Configure the Environment**: Set up your environment, including configuring network settings and creating a database instance.
3. **Connect to the Database**: Use tools like Oracle SQL*Plus or Oracle SQL Developer to connect to your database and start executing SQL commands.
4. **Learn SQL and PL/SQL**: Familiarize yourself with SQL for querying data and PL/SQL for writing procedural code.

1.7 Conclusion

Oracle Database is a powerful tool for managing and utilizing data effectively. With its extensive features and robust architecture, it provides the foundation for various applications and systems. In the following chapters, we will delve deeper into Oracle Database concepts and practical applications, helping you build a solid understanding and proficiency in using this essential database system.

Chapter 2: Setting Up Your Oracle Environment

2.1 Installation of Oracle Database

Setting up Oracle Database is the first step towards leveraging its powerful features. This section will guide you through the installation process on different operating systems.

2.1.1 Downloading Oracle Database

1. **Visit the Oracle Website**: Go to the Oracle Technology Network (OTN) or Oracle Software Delivery Cloud to download the database software.
2. **Choose the Correct Version**: Select the version of Oracle Database that suits your needs. Oracle offers various editions, such as the Oracle Database Express Edition (XE) for beginners, and more advanced editions like the Standard or Enterprise Editions.
3. **Download the Software**: Download the installation package compatible with your operating system (e.g., Windows, Linux). You may need to register for a free Oracle account if you don't already have one.

2.1.2 Installing Oracle Database on Windows

1. **Extract the Installation Files**: Unzip the downloaded package to a directory of your choice.
2. **Run the Installer**: Navigate to the extracted folder and double-click on setup.exe to launch the Oracle Universal Installer.
3. **Follow the Installation Wizard**:
    - **Select Installation Type**: Choose between "Create and configure a database" or "Install database software only."
    - **Specify Oracle Home Location**: Choose or create a directory where Oracle will be installed.
    - **Configure Global Settings**: Set parameters like Oracle Base and Oracle Home.
    - **Choose Database Configuration**: If creating a database, select the configuration options (e.g., typical or advanced).
    - **Provide Database Information**: Enter details such as the database name, passwords, and configuration options.
    - **Review and Install**: Review the settings and click "Install" to start the installation process. Follow the on-screen instructions.

4. **Complete the Installation**: After installation, you will need to configure environment variables and ensure that Oracle services are running.

2.1.3 Installing Oracle Database on Linux

1. **Extract the Installation Files**: Unzip the downloaded package using `unzip` command.
2. **Run the Installer**: Open a terminal, navigate to the directory with the extracted files, and run the `runInstaller` script.
3. **Follow the Installation Wizard**:
    - **Select Installation Type**: Choose whether to create a new database or install software only.
    - **Specify Oracle Home Location**: Define the installation directory.
    - **Configure System Settings**: Input necessary configuration details like global settings and database configuration.
    - **Execute the Installation**: Follow the prompts to complete the installation.
4. **Post-Installation Tasks**: Configure environment variables, set up listeners, and ensure the database service is running.

2.2 Configuration Basics

After installing Oracle Database, you need to configure it to ensure proper functionality and connectivity.

2.2.1 Setting Up the Listener

1. **Access Oracle Net Manager**: Open Oracle Net Manager from the Oracle Home directory.
2. **Configure Listener**:
    - **Add Listener**: Go to the "Listeners" section and add a new listener.
    - **Specify Listener Details**: Enter the listener name, protocol (typically TCP), and port number (default is 1521).
    - **Start the Listener**: Apply the configuration and start the listener.
3. **Verify Listener Configuration**: Use the lsnrctl command-line tool to check the status of the listener.

2.2.2 Creating a Database Instance

1. **Run Database Configuration Assistant (DBCA)**: Open DBCA from the Oracle Home directory.
2. **Select Database Creation Mode**: Choose between creating a new database or configuring an existing one.
3. **Provide Database Information**:
    - **Specify Database Name and SID**: Enter the database name and System Identifier (SID).
    - **Set Administrative Passwords**: Define passwords for administrative accounts such as SYS and SYSTEM.

- - **Configure Storage Options**: Set options for data storage and file locations.
4. **Review and Create**: Review the configuration settings and start the database creation process.
5. **Verify Database Creation**: Check that the database instance is running and accessible.

2.3 Connecting to the Database

Once the database is installed and configured, you need to connect to it to start interacting with it.

2.3.1 Using SQL*Plus

1. **Open SQL*Plus**: Launch SQL*Plus from the command line or through Oracle's application menu.
2. **Connect to the Database**:
    - **Enter Connection Details**: Provide the username, password, and database connection string.
    - **Example Command**:

    sqlplus username/password@hostname:port/SID

3. **Execute SQL Commands**: After connecting, you can start executing SQL queries and commands.

2.3.2 Using Oracle SQL Developer

1. **Launch SQL Developer**: Open Oracle SQL Developer, which provides a graphical interface for database management.
2. **Create a New Connection**:
    - **Specify Connection Details**: Enter the connection name, username, password, and connection type.
    - **Test Connection**: Use the "Test" button to verify the connection settings.
3. **Connect and Manage**: Once the connection is established, you can run SQL queries, manage database objects, and perform various tasks.

2.4 Troubleshooting Common Issues

2.4.1 Installation Problems

- **Check Logs**: Review the installation logs for error messages.
- **Verify System Requirements**: Ensure your system meets the minimum requirements for Oracle Database.
- **Consult Documentation**: Refer to Oracle's installation guides for troubleshooting steps.

2.4.2 Connection Issues

- **Verify Listener Status**: Ensure the Oracle listener is running and configured correctly.
- **Check Firewall Settings**: Ensure that firewall settings are not blocking the database connection.
- **Review Connection Strings**: Double-check the connection details and syntax.

2.5 Conclusion

Setting up Oracle Database is the foundational step towards harnessing its capabilities. By following the installation and configuration steps outlined in this chapter, you'll establish a robust environment for database management and development. In the upcoming chapters, we'll explore Oracle Database architecture, SQL queries, and other essential topics to help you build a solid understanding of how to work with Oracle effectively.

Chapter 3: Understanding Oracle Architecture

3.1 Overview of Oracle Architecture

Understanding Oracle Database architecture is crucial for effectively managing and optimizing the system. Oracle's architecture is designed to ensure high performance, scalability, and reliability. This chapter will break down the key components and their roles within the Oracle Database environment.

3.2 Key Components of Oracle Architecture

3.2.1 Oracle Instance

An Oracle instance is a set of background processes and memory structures that manage the database. It acts as the intermediary between the database and the user's applications. The Oracle instance is composed of two main components:

1. **System Global Area (SGA):**
    - **Definition**: The SGA is a shared memory area used by Oracle processes. It contains data and control information that is shared among all server processes.

- **Components**:
  - **Database Buffer Cache**: Stores copies of data blocks read from the database. It improves performance by reducing the number of disk reads.
  - **Shared Pool**: Contains SQL statements, PL/SQL code, and data dictionary information. It helps in managing SQL execution and parsing.
  - **Redo Log Buffer**: Stores redo entries generated by database changes. It ensures that changes can be recovered in case of a failure.
  - **Large Pool**: Used for memory-intensive operations, such as backup and restore operations, and for session memory.

2. **Background Processes**:
   - **Database Writer (DBWn)**: Responsible for writing data blocks from the buffer cache to the data files on disk.
   - **Log Writer (LGWR)**: Writes redo log entries from the redo log buffer to the online redo log files.
   - **System Monitor (SMON)**: Performs instance recovery and cleans up temporary segments.

- **Process Monitor (PMON)**: Cleans up after failed processes and manages resources.
- **Checkpoint (CKPT)**: Updates data file headers and control files with the latest checkpoint information.
- **Archiver (ARCn)**: Copies online redo log files to archive log files for backup purposes (in ARCHIVELOG mode).

3.2.2 Oracle Database

The Oracle Database is a collection of files that store the actual data, metadata, and control information. It is made up of several key file types:

1. **Data Files**:
   - **Definition**: Data files store user data, including tables, indexes, and clusters. They are the primary storage for all database objects.
   - **Structure**: Each data file is associated with a tablespace, which is a logical storage unit.
2. **Control Files**:
   - **Definition**: Control files contain metadata about the physical structure of the database. They include information about data files, redo log files, and database checkpoints.

- **Importance**: Control files are crucial for database recovery. They are updated by the Oracle instance during database operations.
3. **Redo Log Files**:
    - **Definition**: Redo log files store a record of all changes made to the database. They are used to ensure data integrity and support recovery operations.
    - **Online Redo Logs**: These files are used for active transactions and are overwritten in a cyclic manner.
    - **Archived Redo Logs**: These are copies of online redo logs created for backup purposes when the database is in ARCHIVELOG mode.
4. **Parameter Files (PFILE and SPFILE)**:
    - **Definition**: Parameter files store initialization parameters that configure the Oracle instance.
    - **PFILE**: A text-based parameter file used for initializing the instance.
    - **SPFILE**: A binary parameter file that allows dynamic changes to initialization parameters.

3.3 Oracle Instance vs. Database

Understanding the distinction between an Oracle instance and the Oracle Database is essential:

- **Oracle Instance**: Refers to the set of processes and memory structures that manage the database. It is temporary and can be started or stopped independently of the database.
- **Oracle Database**: Refers to the physical storage of data files, control files, and redo log files. The database is a permanent entity that stores and retrieves data.

3.4 Tablespaces and Segments

3.4.1 Tablespaces

- **Definition**: A tablespace is a logical storage unit within the Oracle Database. It groups related data files together to manage storage efficiently.
- **Types of Tablespaces**:
    - **SYSTEM Tablespace**: Contains data dictionary tables and is required for the database to function.
    - **SYSAUX Tablespace**: An auxiliary tablespace that stores data for various Oracle features and components.
    - **USER Tablespaces**: Used to store user data, such as tables and indexes. These tablespaces can be created by users based on their needs.

3.4.2 Segments

- **Definition**: Segments are physical storage structures within tablespaces. They represent the storage space allocated to database objects.
- **Types of Segments**:
    - **Data Segments**: Store data for tables or clusters.
    - **Index Segments**: Store data for indexes.
    - **Temporary Segments**: Used for sorting and temporary storage during operations.
    - **Rollback Segments**: Used to manage data consistency and rollback operations (replaced by undo segments in newer versions).

3.5 Data Dictionary Views

Data dictionary views are built-in views that provide information about the database's structure and objects. These views are essential for querying metadata and understanding database components.

- **V$ Views**: Dynamic performance views that provide real-time information about the database instance, such as V$SESSION, V$SQL, and V$DATABASE.
- **ALL_, DBA_, and USER_ Views**: Provide information about database objects accessible to

users, all objects, and objects owned by the current user, respectively.

3.6 Oracle Architecture Summary

Oracle Database architecture is a well-organized system designed to manage data efficiently and reliably. The architecture comprises the Oracle instance, database files, tablespaces, and various background processes. Understanding these components and their roles will help you manage and optimize your Oracle Database environment effectively.

In the next chapter, we will delve into basic SQL queries, which are essential for interacting with and manipulating data in Oracle Database.

Chapter 4: Basic SQL Queries

SQL (Structured Query Language) is the standard language for managing and manipulating databases. In this chapter, we will explore the basics of SQL queries, which are fundamental for interacting with Oracle Database. Understanding these basics will enable you to retrieve, insert, update, and delete data within your database.

4.1 Introduction to SQL

SQL is a powerful language used to perform various operations on the data stored in a relational database. It is used to query data, modify data, and control access to data. The primary SQL operations include querying data (SELECT), inserting data (INSERT), updating data (UPDATE), and deleting data (DELETE).

4.2 The SELECT Statement

The SELECT statement is used to retrieve data from one or more tables in a database. It is the most commonly used SQL command.

4.2.1 Basic SELECT Query

To select data from a table, you use the SELECT statement followed by the column names you want to retrieve and the FROM clause specifying the table name.

Syntax:

```
SELECT column1, column2, ...
FROM table_name;
```

Example:

```
SELECT first_name, last_name
FROM employees;
```

This query retrieves the first_name and last_name columns from the employees table.

4.2.2 Selecting All Columns

To select all columns from a table, you can use the asterisk (*) wildcard.

Syntax:

```
SELECT *
FROM table_name;
```

Example:

```
SELECT *
FROM employees;
```

This query retrieves all columns from the employees table.

4.2.3 Filtering Data with WHERE Clause

The WHERE clause is used to filter records based on specified conditions.

Syntax:

```
SELECT column1, column2, ...
FROM table_name
WHERE condition;
```

Example:

```
SELECT first_name, last_name
FROM employees
WHERE department_id = 10;
```

This query retrieves the first_name and last_name of employees who belong to department 10.

4.2.4 Sorting Results with ORDER BY Clause

The ORDER BY clause is used to sort the result set by one or more columns.

Syntax:

```
SELECT column1, column2, ...
FROM table_name
ORDER BY column1 [ASC|DESC];
```

Example:

```
SELECT first_name, last_name
FROM employees
ORDER BY last_name ASC;
```

This query retrieves the first_name and last_name columns from the employees table and sorts the results by last_name in ascending order.

4.3 The INSERT Statement

The INSERT statement is used to add new rows to a table.

4.3.1 Inserting Data into a Table

Syntax:

```
INSERT INTO table_name (column1, column2, ...)
VALUES (value1, value2, ...);
```

Example:

```
INSERT INTO employees (first_name, last_name, department_id)
VALUES ('John', 'Doe', 10);
```

This query inserts a new row into the employees table with the specified values for first_name, last_name, and department_id.

4.3.2 Inserting Multiple Rows

You can also insert multiple rows in a single INSERT statement.

Syntax:

```
INSERT INTO table_name (column1, column2, ...)
VALUES (value1, value2, ...),
    (value3, value4, ...),
    ...;
```

Example:

```
INSERT INTO employees (first_name, last_name, department_id)
VALUES ('Jane', 'Smith', 20),
    ('Emily', 'Jones', 30);
```

This query inserts two new rows into the employees table.

4.4 The UPDATE Statement

The UPDATE statement is used to modify existing rows in a table.

Syntax:

```
UPDATE table_name
SET column1 = value1, column2 = value2, ...
WHERE condition;
```

Example:

```
UPDATE employees
SET department_id = 20
WHERE employee_id = 101;
```

This query updates the department_id to 20 for the employee with employee_id 101.

4.5 The DELETE Statement

The DELETE statement is used to remove rows from a table.

Syntax:

```
DELETE FROM table_name
WHERE condition;
```

Example:

```
DELETE FROM employees
WHERE employee_id = 101;
```

This query deletes the row from the employees table where employee_id is 101.

4.5.1 Deleting All Rows

To delete all rows from a table without removing the table structure, you can omit the WHERE clause.

Example:

DELETE FROM employees;

This query removes all rows from the employees table but leaves the table structure intact.

4.6 Using SQL Functions

SQL functions can be used to perform operations on data during queries. Some common functions include:

4.6.1 Aggregate Functions

- **COUNT()**: Returns the number of rows.
- **SUM()**: Returns the sum of a numeric column.
- **AVG()**: Returns the average value of a numeric column.
- **MAX()**: Returns the maximum value in a column.
- **MIN()**: Returns the minimum value in a column.

Example:

```
SELECT department_id, COUNT(*)
FROM employees
GROUP BY department_id;
```

This query counts the number of employees in each department.

4.6.2 String Functions

- **CONCAT()**: Concatenates two or more strings.
- **UPPER()**: Converts a string to uppercase.
- **LOWER()**: Converts a string to lowercase.
- **LENGTH()**: Returns the length of a string.

Example:

```
SELECT UPPER(first_name)
FROM employees;
```

This query converts the first_name column to uppercase.

4.7 Joining Tables

SQL joins are used to combine rows from two or more tables based on a related column.

4.7.1 INNER JOIN

An INNER JOIN returns rows when there is a match in both tables.

Syntax:

```
SELECT columns
FROM table1
INNER JOIN table2
ON table1.common_column = table2.common_column;
```

Example:

```
SELECT employees.first_name, departments.department_name
FROM employees
INNER JOIN departments
ON employees.department_id = departments.department_id;
```

This query retrieves employee names along with their department names.

4.7.2 LEFT JOIN

A LEFT JOIN returns all rows from the left table and matched rows from the right table. Non-matching rows from the right table are returned as NULL.

Syntax:

```
SELECT columns
FROM table1
LEFT JOIN table2
ON table1.common_column = table2.common_column;
```

Example:

```
SELECT employees.first_name, departments.department_name
FROM employees
LEFT JOIN departments
ON employees.department_id = departments.department_id;
```

This query retrieves all employees and their department names, showing NULL for employees without a department.

4.8 Conclusion

Understanding basic SQL queries is essential for managing and interacting with Oracle Database. This chapter covered fundamental SQL operations, including retrieving, inserting, updating, and deleting data. We also explored SQL functions and joins, which enhance the ability to manipulate and analyze data. In the next chapter, we will delve into database objects and structures, providing a deeper understanding of how data is organized and managed in Oracle Database.

Chapter 5: Database Objects and Structures

In Oracle Database, data is organized and managed using various objects and structures. Understanding these objects is crucial for designing and maintaining an efficient database. This chapter will cover the fundamental database objects, their purposes, and how they interact within the Oracle environment.

5.1 Tables

5.1.1 Definition

A table is the primary database object where data is stored. It consists of rows and columns, where each row represents a record, and each column represents an attribute of that record.

5.1.2 Creating a Table

To create a table, you use the CREATE TABLE statement, specifying the table name and the columns along with their data types.

Syntax:

```
CREATE TABLE table_name (
    column1 data_type [constraints],
    column2 data_type [constraints],
    ...
);
```

Example:

```
CREATE TABLE employees (
    employee_id NUMBER PRIMARY KEY,
    first_name VARCHAR2(50),
    last_name VARCHAR2(50),
    department_id NUMBER,
    hire_date DATE
);
```

This query creates an employees table with columns for employee ID, first name, last name, department ID, and hire date.

5.1.3 Modifying a Table

You can modify a table structure using the ALTER TABLE statement. This includes adding, dropping, or modifying columns.

Syntax:

```
ALTER TABLE table_name
ADD (new_column data_type);
```

Example:

```
ALTER TABLE employees
ADD (email VARCHAR2(100));
```

This query adds a new email column to the employees table.

5.2 Indexes

5.2.1 Definition

An index is a database object that improves the speed of data retrieval operations. It creates a data structure that allows for faster searches on columns.

5.2.2 Creating an Index

Syntax:

```
CREATE INDEX index_name
ON table_name (column1, column2, ...);
```

Example:

```
CREATE INDEX idx_last_name
ON employees (last_name);
```

This query creates an index on the last_name column of the employees table, enhancing the performance of queries that search by last name.

5.2.3 Dropping an Index

To remove an index, you use the DROP INDEX statement.

Syntax:

```
DROP INDEX index_name;
```

Example:

```
DROP INDEX idx_last_name;
```

This query drops the idx_last_name index.

5.3 Views

5.3.1 Definition

A view is a virtual table that provides a specific representation of data from one or more tables. It does not store data itself but presents a filtered or summarized view of the data.

5.3.2 Creating a View

Syntax:

```
CREATE VIEW view_name AS
SELECT column1, column2, ...
FROM table_name
WHERE condition;
```

Example:

```
CREATE VIEW employee_view AS
SELECT first_name, last_name, department_id
FROM employees
WHERE hire_date > '2023-01-01';
```

This query creates a view named employee_view showing employees hired after January 1, 2023.

5.3.3 Querying a View

You can query a view just like a regular table.

Example:

```
SELECT * FROM employee_view;
```

This query retrieves all data from the employee_view.

5.3.4 Dropping a View

To remove a view, use the DROP VIEW statement.

Syntax: DROP VIEW view_name;

Example:

```
DROP VIEW employee_view;
```

This query drops the employee_view.

5.4 Constraints

5.4.1 Definition

Constraints are rules applied to table columns to ensure data integrity and consistency. Common constraints include primary keys, foreign keys, unique constraints, and check constraints.

5.4.2 Primary Key Constraint

A primary key uniquely identifies each row in a table and cannot contain NULL values.

Syntax:

PRIMARY KEY (column1, column2, ...)

Example:

```
CREATE TABLE employees (
    employee_id NUMBER PRIMARY KEY,
    first_name VARCHAR2(50),
    last_name VARCHAR2(50)
);
```

5.4.3 Foreign Key Constraint

A foreign key establishes a relationship between two tables by linking a column in one table to the primary key of another table.

Syntax:

```
FOREIGN KEY (column)
REFERENCES parent_table (parent_column)
```

Example:

```
CREATE TABLE departments (
    department_id NUMBER PRIMARY KEY,
    department_name VARCHAR2(50)
);

CREATE TABLE employees (
    employee_id NUMBER PRIMARY KEY,
    first_name VARCHAR2(50),
    last_name VARCHAR2(50),
    department_id NUMBER,
    FOREIGN KEY (department_id) REFERENCES departments(department_id)
);
```

This query creates a foreign key on the department_id column in the employees table, referencing the department_id column in the departments table.

5.4.4 Unique Constraint

A unique constraint ensures that all values in a column are distinct.

Syntax:

```
UNIQUE (column)
```

Example:

```
CREATE TABLE employees (
    employee_id NUMBER PRIMARY KEY,
    email VARCHAR2(100) UNIQUE
);
```

This query ensures that each email value in the employees table is unique.

5.4.5 Check Constraint

A check constraint enforces a condition on values in a column.

Syntax:

```
CHECK (condition)
```

Example:

```
CREATE TABLE employees (
    employee_id NUMBER PRIMARY KEY,
    salary NUMBER CHECK (salary > 0)
);
```

This query ensures that the salary column contains only positive values.

5.5 Tablespaces

5.5.1 Definition

A tablespace is a logical storage unit that groups related data files. It helps in managing and organizing database storage.

5.5.2 Creating a Tablespace

Syntax:

```
CREATE TABLESPACE tablespace_name
DATAFILE 'file_path' SIZE size;
```

Example:

```
CREATE TABLESPACE users
DATAFILE '/path_to_file/users01.dbf' SIZE 100M;
```

This query creates a tablespace named users with a data file of 100 MB.

5.5.3 Altering a Tablespace

You can modify tablespace attributes using the ALTER TABLESPACE statement.

Syntax:

```
ALTER TABLESPACE tablespace_name
ADD DATAFILE 'file_path' SIZE size;
```

Example:

```
ALTER TABLESPACE users
ADD DATAFILE '/path_to_file/users02.dbf' SIZE 100M;
```

This query adds an additional data file to the users tablespace.

5.5.4 Dropping a Tablespace

To remove a tablespace, use the DROP TABLESPACE statement. You can also include the INCLUDING CONTENTS option to delete all associated data files.

Syntax:

```
DROP TABLESPACE tablespace_name INCLUDING CONTENTS;
```

Example:

```
DROP TABLESPACE users INCLUDING CONTENTS;
```

This query drops the users tablespace and deletes all associated data files.

5.6 Synonyms

5.6.1 Definition

A synonym is an alias for a database object, such as a table, view, or sequence. It simplifies access to objects and can be used to hide the object's complexity.

5.6.2 Creating a Synonym

Syntax:

```
CREATE SYNONYM synonym_name
FOR schema.object_name;
```

Example:

```
CREATE SYNONYM emp FOR hr.employees;
```

This query creates a synonym emp for the employees table in the hr schema.

5.6.3 Dropping a Synonym

To remove a synonym, use the DROP SYNONYM statement.

Syntax:

```
DROP SYNONYM synonym_name;
```

Example:

```
DROP SYNONYM emp;
```

This query drops the emp synonym.

5.7 Conclusion

Understanding database objects and structures is fundamental to effectively managing and designing an Oracle Database. In this chapter, we covered the essential objects like tables, indexes, views, constraints, tablespaces, and synonyms. Mastering these concepts will help you organize and manipulate data efficiently in Oracle Database. In the next chapter, we will delve into more advanced SQL techniques and query optimization strategies to further enhance your database skills.

Chapter 6: Advanced SQL Techniques and Query Optimization

In Oracle Database, mastering advanced SQL techniques and query optimization is essential for ensuring high performance and efficient data retrieval. This chapter will explore advanced SQL concepts and optimization strategies to enhance your ability to work with large datasets and complex queries.

6.1 Advanced SQL Techniques

6.1.1 Subqueries

A subquery is a query nested inside another query. Subqueries can be used in various parts of a SQL statement, such as the SELECT, WHERE, or FROM clauses, to provide intermediate results for the main query.

Syntax:

```
SELECT column1, column2
FROM table_name
WHERE column1 = (SELECT column1 FROM table_name WHERE condition);
```

Example:

```
SELECT first_name, last_name
FROM employees
WHERE department_id = (SELECT department_id FROM
departments WHERE department_name = 'Sales');
```

This query retrieves employees who work in the 'Sales' department by using a subquery to find the department ID.

6.1.2 Joins

In addition to basic joins, Oracle supports advanced join techniques:

1. **Self Join**: A join of a table with itself. Useful for hierarchical data or comparing rows within the same table.

Example:

```
SELECT e1.first_name AS Employee, e2.first_name AS Manager
FROM employees e1
JOIN employees e2 ON e1.manager_id = e2.employee_id;
```

This query retrieves employees and their managers from the employees table.

Outer Join: Retrieves records that have no matching rows in other tables (e.g., LEFT JOIN, RIGHT JOIN).

Example:

```
SELECT e.first_name, d.department_name
FROM employees e
LEFT JOIN departments d ON e.department_id = d.department_id;
```

This query retrieves all employees and their department names, including employees who do not belong to any department.

6.1.3 Set Operations

Set operations combine the results of two or more queries. Common set operations include:

1. **UNION**: Combines results from multiple queries and removes duplicates.

Syntax:

```
SELECT column1 FROM table1
UNION
SELECT column1 FROM table2;
```

Example:

```
SELECT first_name FROM employees
UNION
SELECT first_name FROM contractors;
```

This query retrieves unique first names from both the employees and contractors tables.

2. **INTERSECT**: Returns only the rows that are present in both queries.

Syntax:

```
SELECT column1 FROM table1
INTERSECT
SELECT column1 FROM table2;
```

Example:

```
SELECT department_id FROM employees
INTERSECT
SELECT department_id FROM departments;
```

This query retrieves department IDs that are present in both the employees and departments tables.

3. **MINUS**: Returns rows from the first query that are not present in the second query.

Syntax:

```
SELECT column1 FROM table1
MINUS
SELECT column1 FROM table2;
```

Example:

```
SELECT employee_id FROM employees
MINUS
SELECT employee_id FROM terminated_employees;
```

This query retrieves employee IDs from the employees table that are not present in the terminated_employees table.

6.2 Query Optimization

Optimizing queries is essential for improving performance and reducing execution time. This section will cover common techniques for query optimization.

6.2.1 Indexing

Indexes improve query performance by allowing faster data retrieval. When creating indexes, consider the following:

1. **Choose the Right Columns**: Index columns that are frequently used in WHERE, JOIN, and ORDER BY clauses.
2. **Avoid Over-Indexing**: Too many indexes can slow down INSERT, UPDATE, and DELETE operations.

Example:

```sql
CREATE INDEX idx_emp_dept ON employees (department_id);
```

This query creates an index on the department_id column of the employees table to improve performance for queries involving this column.

6.2.2 Query Execution Plans

The execution plan shows how Oracle executes a SQL query. Analyzing the execution plan helps identify performance bottlenecks.

To view an execution plan:

```
EXPLAIN PLAN FOR
SELECT first_name, last_name
FROM employees
WHERE department_id = 10;
```

Querying the execution plan:

SELECT * FROM table(dbms_xplan.display);

6.2.3 Optimizing Joins

Joins can be optimized by:

1. **Using Proper Join Types**: Choose the most efficient join type (e.g., INNER JOIN over OUTER JOIN) based on your query requirements.
2. **Filtering Early**: Apply filters as early as possible to reduce the number of rows processed in joins.

Example:

```
SELECT e.first_name, d.department_name
FROM employees e
JOIN departments d ON e.department_id = d.department_id
WHERE e.hire_date > '2023-01-01';
```

This query applies the filter on hire_date before performing the join, optimizing performance.

6.2.4 Avoiding Full Table Scans

A full table scan reads all rows from a table, which can be inefficient. To avoid full table scans:

1. **Use Indexes**: Ensure that indexes are used for queries with selective conditions.
2. **Limit Results**: Use LIMIT or ROWNUM to restrict the number of rows retrieved.

Example:

```
SELECT first_name, last_name
FROM employees
WHERE department_id = 10
AND ROWNUM <= 100;
```

This query retrieves a maximum of 100 rows for employees in department 10.

6.3 SQL Tuning Tips

1. **Analyze and Gather Statistics**: Regularly gather statistics on tables and indexes to help Oracle's optimizer make better decisions.

Example:

```
EXEC DBMS_STATS.GATHER_TABLE_STATS('schema_name', 'table_name');
```

2. **Use Bind Variables**: Bind variables can improve query performance by reducing the need for repeated parsing.

Example:

```
SELECT first_name, last_name
FROM employees
WHERE department_id = :dept_id;
```

3. **Optimize Subqueries**: Ensure subqueries are efficient and consider using joins or common table expressions (CTEs) for better performance.

Example:

```
WITH dept_employees AS (
```

```
    SELECT employee_id
    FROM employees
    WHERE department_id = 10
)
SELECT e.first_name, e.last_name
FROM employees e
JOIN dept_employees de ON e.employee_id = de.employee_id;
```

6.4 Conclusion

Advanced SQL techniques and query optimization are essential for managing and querying data efficiently in Oracle Database. This chapter covered subqueries, advanced joins, set operations, indexing, execution plans, and various optimization strategies. Applying these techniques will help you write more efficient queries and enhance the overall performance of your database. In the next chapter, we will explore Oracle PL/SQL, a powerful extension of SQL for procedural programming.

Chapter 7: Introduction to PL/SQL

PL/SQL (Procedural Language/SQL) is Oracle's procedural extension for SQL, providing a way to write complex queries and operations in a structured manner. It combines the power of SQL with the procedural capabilities of a programming language, allowing for advanced data manipulation and control-flow operations. In this chapter, we will introduce you to PL/SQL, covering its fundamental features and providing practical examples.

7.1 Understanding PL/SQL

7.1.1 What is PL/SQL?

PL/SQL is a procedural extension to SQL developed by Oracle. It allows for the creation of complex applications, including stored procedures, functions, triggers, and packages. PL/SQL provides features like variables, conditional statements, loops, and exception handling, which are not available in standard SQL.

7.1.2 PL/SQL Block Structure

PL/SQL programs are written in blocks, which are the fundamental units of execution. A PL/SQL block consists of three main sections:

1. **Declaration Section**: Where you declare variables, constants, and cursors.
2. **Execution Section**: Where you write the code that performs the main operations.
3. **Exception Handling Section**: Where you handle runtime errors and exceptions.

Syntax:

```
DECLARE
  -- Declaration section
BEGIN
  -- Execution section
EXCEPTION
  -- Exception handling section
END;
```

Example:

```
DECLARE
  v_employee_name VARCHAR2(50);
BEGIN
  v_employee_name := 'John Doe';
  DBMS_OUTPUT.PUT_LINE('Employee Name: ' || v_employee_name);
EXCEPTION
  WHEN OTHERS THEN
    DBMS_OUTPUT.PUT_LINE('An error occurred.');
END;
```

7.2 Variables and Data Types

7.2.1 Declaring Variables

Variables in PL/SQL are used to store data temporarily during program execution. They are declared in the declaration section of a PL/SQL block.

Syntax:

```
variable_name data_type [DEFAULT initial_value];
```

Example:

```
DECLARE
  v_employee_id NUMBER := 1001;
  v_employee_name VARCHAR2(50);
BEGIN
  -- Code to use variables
END;
```

7.2.2 PL/SQL Data Types

PL/SQL supports various data types, including:

1. **NUMBER**: For numeric values.
2. **VARCHAR2**: For variable-length character strings.
3. **CHAR**: For fixed-length character strings.
4. **DATE**: For date and time values.
5. **BOOLEAN**: For true/false values.

Example:

```
DECLARE
  v_salary NUMBER(8,2);
  v_hire_date DATE;
  v_is_active BOOLEAN;
BEGIN
  v_salary := 50000.00;
  v_hire_date := SYSDATE;
  v_is_active := TRUE;
END;
```

7.3 Control Structures

7.3.1 Conditional Statements

PL/SQL provides conditional statements to control the flow of execution based on conditions.

1. **IF-THEN-ELSE**:

Syntax:

```
IF condition THEN
    -- Code to execute if condition is true
ELSE
    -- Code to execute if condition is false
END IF;
```

Example:

```
DECLARE
  v_salary NUMBER := 45000;
BEGIN
  IF v_salary > 40000 THEN
    DBMS_OUTPUT.PUT_LINE('Salary is above average.');
  ELSE
    DBMS_OUTPUT.PUT_LINE('Salary is below average.');
  END IF;
END;
```

2. **CASE Statement**:

Syntax:

```
CASE expression
  WHEN value1 THEN
    -- Code to execute if expression equals value1
  WHEN value2 THEN
    -- Code to execute if expression equals value2
  ELSE
    -- Code to execute if no match
END CASE;
```

Example:

```
DECLARE
  v_department_id NUMBER := 10;
BEGIN
  CASE v_department_id
    WHEN 10 THEN
```

```
      DBMS_OUTPUT.PUT_LINE('Sales Department');
    WHEN 20 THEN
      DBMS_OUTPUT.PUT_LINE('Marketing Department');
    ELSE
      DBMS_OUTPUT.PUT_LINE('Unknown Department');
  END CASE;
END;
```

7.3.2 Loops

PL/SQL supports different types of loops for iterative execution:

1. **FOR Loop**:

Syntax:

```
FOR variable IN start_value..end_value LOOP
   -- Code to execute
END LOOP;
```

Example:

```
DECLARE
  v_i NUMBER;
BEGIN
  FOR v_i IN 1..5 LOOP
    DBMS_OUTPUT.PUT_LINE('Iteration: ' || v_i);
  END LOOP;
END;
```

2. **WHILE Loop**:

Syntax:

```
WHILE condition LOOP
  -- Code to execute
END LOOP;
```

Example:

```
DECLARE
  v_counter NUMBER := 1;
BEGIN
  WHILE v_counter <= 5 LOOP
    DBMS_OUTPUT.PUT_LINE('Counter: ' || v_counter);
    v_counter := v_counter + 1;
  END LOOP;
END;
```

7.4 Cursors

7.4.1 What is a Cursor?

A cursor is a database object that allows you to retrieve and manipulate data row by row. Cursors are used to process query results one row at a time.

7.4.2 Implicit Cursors

Implicit cursors are automatically created by Oracle for single SQL statements. They are useful for simple queries.

Example:

```
BEGIN
  SELECT COUNT(*) INTO v_count FROM employees;
  DBMS_OUTPUT.PUT_LINE('Total Employees: ' || v_count);
END;
```

7.4.3 Explicit Cursors

Explicit cursors are defined by the programmer and offer more control over query processing.

Syntax:

```
DECLARE
  CURSOR cursor_name IS
    SELECT_statement;
  variable_name cursor_name%ROWTYPE;
BEGIN
  OPEN cursor_name;
  FETCH cursor_name INTO variable_name;
  CLOSE cursor_name;
END;
```

Example:

```
DECLARE
  CURSOR emp_cursor IS
    SELECT first_name, last_name FROM employees;
  v_employee emp_cursor%ROWTYPE;
BEGIN
  OPEN emp_cursor;
  LOOP
    FETCH emp_cursor INTO v_employee;
    EXIT WHEN emp_cursor%NOTFOUND;
    DBMS_OUTPUT.PUT_LINE(v_employee.first_name || ' ' || v_employee.last_name);
  END LOOP;
  CLOSE emp_cursor;
END;
```

7.5 Exception Handling

7.5.1 What is Exception Handling?

Exception handling allows you to manage runtime errors and handle exceptional conditions gracefully.

7.5.2 Predefined Exceptions

Oracle provides predefined exceptions for common error conditions, such as NO_DATA_FOUND, TOO_MANY_ROWS, and ZERO_DIVIDE.

Example:

```
BEGIN
  -- Code that may raise an exception
EXCEPTION
  WHEN NO_DATA_FOUND THEN
    DBMS_OUTPUT.PUT_LINE('No data found.');
  WHEN TOO_MANY_ROWS THEN
    DBMS_OUTPUT.PUT_LINE('Query returned more than one row.');
  WHEN OTHERS THEN
    DBMS_OUTPUT.PUT_LINE('An unexpected error occurred.');
END;
```

7.5.3 User-Defined Exceptions

You can define your own exceptions for specific error conditions.

Syntax:

```
DECLARE
  my_exception EXCEPTION;
BEGIN
  -- Code that raises my_exception
EXCEPTION
  WHEN my_exception THEN
    DBMS_OUTPUT.PUT_LINE('Custom exception occurred.');
END;
```

Example:

```
DECLARE
  invalid_salary EXCEPTION;
  v_salary NUMBER := -5000;
BEGIN
  IF v_salary < 0 THEN
    RAISE invalid_salary;
  END IF;
EXCEPTION
  WHEN invalid_salary THEN
    DBMS_OUTPUT.PUT_LINE('Invalid salary amount.');
END;
```

7.6 Procedures and Functions

7.6.1 Stored Procedures

A stored procedure is a named PL/SQL block that performs a specific task and can be executed on demand.

Syntax:

```
CREATE OR REPLACE PROCEDURE procedure_name (parameters) IS
BEGIN
   -- Procedure code
END procedure_name;
```

Example:

```
CREATE OR REPLACE PROCEDURE greet_employee (p_name IN
VARCHAR2) IS
BEGIN
  DBMS_OUTPUT.PUT_LINE('Hello, ' || p_name || '!');
END greet_employee;
```

7.6.2 Stored Functions

A stored function is similar to a procedure but returns a value.

Syntax:

```
CREATE OR REPLACE FUNCTION function_name (parameters)
RETURN return_type IS
BEGIN
  -- Function code
  RETURN value;
END function_name;
```

Example:

```
CREATE OR REPLACE FUNCTION get_employee_salary
(p_employee_id IN NUMBER) RETURN NUMBER IS
  v_salary NUMBER;
BEGIN
  SELECT salary INTO v_salary FROM employees WHERE
employee_id = p_employee_id;
  RETURN v_salary;
END get_employee_salary;
```

7.7 Packages

7.7.1 What is a Package?

A package is a collection of related procedures, functions, variables, and cursors. Packages provide modularity and encapsulation.

7.7.2 Creating a Package

Syntax:

```
CREATE OR REPLACE PACKAGE package_name AS
  -- Public declarations
END package_name;
```

Example:

```
CREATE OR REPLACE PACKAGE employee_pkg AS
   PROCEDURE greet_employee (p_name IN VARCHAR2);
   FUNCTION get_employee_salary (p_employee_id IN NUMBER)
RETURN NUMBER;
END employee_pkg;
```

7.7.3 Creating a Package Body

The package body contains the implementation of the package's procedures and functions.

Syntax:

```
CREATE OR REPLACE PACKAGE BODY package_name AS
   PROCEDURE procedure_name IS
   BEGIN
      -- Procedure code
   END procedure_name;

   FUNCTION function_name RETURN return_type IS
   BEGIN
      -- Function code
      RETURN value;
   END function_name;
END package_name;
```

Example:

```
CREATE OR REPLACE PACKAGE BODY employee_pkg AS
  PROCEDURE greet_employee (p_name IN VARCHAR2) IS
  BEGIN
    DBMS_OUTPUT.PUT_LINE('Hello, ' || p_name || '!');
  END greet_employee;

  FUNCTION get_employee_salary (p_employee_id IN NUMBER) RETURN NUMBER IS
    v_salary NUMBER;
  BEGIN
    SELECT salary INTO v_salary FROM employees WHERE employee_id = p_employee_id;
    RETURN v_salary;
  END get_employee_salary;
END employee_pkg;
```

7.8 Conclusion

PL/SQL is a powerful tool for extending SQL with procedural programming capabilities, enabling the development of complex database applications. In this chapter, we introduced the basics of PL/SQL, including its block structure, variables, control structures, cursors, exception handling, and modular programming with procedures, functions, and packages. Mastering these concepts will allow you to write more efficient and maintainable database applications. In the next chapter, we will explore advanced PL/SQL programming techniques and best practices.

Chapter 8: Managing Transactions and Concurrency

In Oracle Database, managing transactions and concurrency is essential for ensuring data integrity and consistency in a multi-user environment. This chapter will cover the fundamentals of transaction management, concurrency control, and strategies for handling transactions in PL/SQL.

8.1 Understanding Transactions

8.1.1 What is a Transaction?

A transaction is a sequence of one or more SQL operations executed as a single unit of work. Transactions ensure that database changes are applied consistently and reliably. The key properties of transactions are encapsulated by the ACID principles:

1. **Atomicity**: Ensures that all operations within a transaction are completed successfully; if any operation fails, the entire transaction is rolled back.

2. **Consistency**: Ensures that the database transitions from one consistent state to another consistent state after a transaction.
3. **Isolation**: Ensures that the operations of a transaction are isolated from other concurrent transactions until the transaction is completed.
4. **Durability**: Ensures that once a transaction is committed, its changes are permanent and survive system failures.

8.1.2 Transaction Control Statements

PL/SQL provides several statements to control transactions:

1. **COMMIT**: Permanently saves all changes made during the transaction.

    Syntax:

    ```
    COMMIT;
    ```

    Example:

    ```
    BEGIN
       UPDATE employees SET salary = salary * 1.10 WHERE department_id = 10;
       COMMIT;
    END;
    ```

2. **ROLLBACK**: Undoes all changes made during the transaction.

   Syntax:

   ```
   ROLLBACK;
   ```

   Example:

   ```
   BEGIN
      UPDATE employees SET salary = salary * 1.10 WHERE department_id = 10;
      ROLLBACK;
   END;
   ```

3. **SAVEPOINT**: Sets a point within a transaction to which you can roll back.

   Syntax:

   ```
   SAVEPOINT savepoint_name;
   ```

Example:

```
BEGIN
   UPDATE employees SET salary = salary * 1.10 WHERE department_id = 10;
   SAVEPOINT before_adjustment;
   UPDATE employees SET salary = salary * 0.90 WHERE department_id = 20;
   ROLLBACK TO before_adjustment;
   COMMIT;
END;
```

8.2 Concurrency Control

8.2.1 What is Concurrency Control?

Concurrency control manages simultaneous operations on the database without conflicting with each other. It ensures that transactions are executed in a way that maintains data consistency and integrity.

8.2.2 Locking Mechanisms

Oracle uses locking mechanisms to control concurrent access to data:

1. **Row-Level Locking**: Locks individual rows that are being modified. This minimizes contention and allows multiple transactions to work on different rows of the same table simultaneously.
2. **Table-Level Locking**: Locks entire tables, which can be necessary for certain operations but can lead to higher contention.

Example of Row-Level Locking:

```
BEGIN
  UPDATE employees SET salary = salary * 1.10 WHERE employee_id = 1001;
  COMMIT;
END;
```

Example of Table-Level Locking:

```
BEGIN
  LOCK TABLE employees IN EXCLUSIVE MODE;
  UPDATE employees SET salary = salary * 1.10 WHERE department_id = 10;
  COMMIT;
END;
```

8.2.3 Isolation Levels

Oracle supports different isolation levels that determine the degree of visibility of changes made by one transaction to other concurrent transactions:

1. **READ COMMITTED**: The default isolation level in Oracle. Allows a transaction to see changes committed by other transactions but not changes made by transactions that are still in progress.
2. **SERIALIZABLE**: Provides a higher level of isolation by ensuring that transactions operate in a serial order, making it as if transactions are executed one after another.
3. **READ UNCOMMITTED**: Allows a transaction to see changes made by other transactions even if they are not committed. This is not supported directly in Oracle but can be simulated in certain ways.
4. **REPEATABLE READ**: Ensures that if a transaction reads a row, subsequent reads of the same row will return the same values, even if other transactions modify the row in between.

Example:

```
SET TRANSACTION ISOLATION LEVEL SERIALIZABLE;
BEGIN
  -- Transaction code
  COMMIT;
END;
```

8.3 Handling Deadlocks

8.3.1 What is a Deadlock?

A deadlock occurs when two or more transactions are waiting for each other to release locks, causing a situation where none of the transactions can proceed.

8.3.2 Detecting and Resolving Deadlocks

Oracle automatically detects deadlocks and resolves them by rolling back one of the transactions involved. The application should handle such scenarios gracefully by catching exceptions and possibly retrying the transaction.

Example:

```
BEGIN
   UPDATE employees SET salary = salary * 1.10 WHERE employee_id = 1001;
   COMMIT;
EXCEPTION
   WHEN DEADLOCK DETECTED THEN
     DBMS_OUTPUT.PUT_LINE('A deadlock occurred. Please retry the transaction.');
     ROLLBACK;
END;
```

8.4 Best Practices for Transaction Management

1. **Keep Transactions Short**: Minimize the time transactions hold locks to reduce contention and improve performance.
2. **Use Appropriate Isolation Levels**: Choose the isolation level based on the requirements for data consistency and performance.
3. **Handle Exceptions**: Implement proper exception handling to manage errors and deadlocks effectively.
4. **Test Concurrency Scenarios**: Test your application under concurrent access to identify and address potential issues.

8.5 Conclusion

Effective transaction management and concurrency control are vital for maintaining data integrity and ensuring smooth operations in a multi-user environment. In this chapter, we covered the basics of transactions, concurrency control mechanisms, isolation levels, deadlock handling, and best practices. Understanding these concepts will help you design robust and reliable database applications. In the next chapter, we will delve into Oracle's security features and practices to protect your data and applications.

Chapter 9: Oracle Security Features and Practices

Ensuring the security of your database is crucial for protecting sensitive information and maintaining data integrity. Oracle Database provides a comprehensive set of security features and practices to safeguard your data against unauthorized access and breaches. This chapter will cover essential aspects of Oracle security, including user management, privileges, roles, and data encryption.

9.1 User Management

9.1.1 Creating and Managing Users

In Oracle, users are individuals or applications that access the database. Proper user management ensures that only authorized users have access to the database.

Creating a User:

Syntax:

```
CREATE USER username IDENTIFIED BY password;
```

Example:

```
CREATE USER john_doe IDENTIFIED BY strong_password;
```

Granting Privileges to a User:

Privileges define what actions a user can perform. Common privileges include the ability to query, insert, update, and delete data.

Syntax:

```
GRANT privilege_type ON object TO username;
```

Example:

```
GRANT SELECT, INSERT ON employees TO john_doe;
```

Modifying User Accounts:

To change user passwords or other attributes, use the ALTER USER statement.

Syntax:

```
ALTER USER username IDENTIFIED BY new_password;
```

Example:

```
ALTER USER john_doe IDENTIFIED BY new_strong_password;
```

Dropping a User:

To remove a user from the database, use the DROP USER statement. Be cautious, as this will delete the user and their associated objects.

Syntax:

```
DROP USER username CASCADE;
```

Example:

```
DROP USER john_doe CASCADE;
```

9.2 Privileges and Roles

9.2.1 System and Object Privileges

System Privileges:

System privileges allow users to perform administrative tasks or access certain database features. Examples include CREATE TABLE, CREATE USER, and DROP TABLE.

Syntax:

```
GRANT privilege TO username;
```

Example:

```
GRANT CREATE SESSION TO john_doe;
```

Object Privileges:

Object privileges allow users to perform actions on specific database objects such as tables, views, and procedures. Examples include SELECT, INSERT, UPDATE, and DELETE.

Syntax:

```
GRANT privilege ON object TO username;
```

Example:

```
GRANT SELECT ON employees TO john_doe;
```

9.2.2 Roles

Roles are named collections of privileges that can be granted to users. Roles simplify privilege management and allow for easier administration.

Creating a Role:

Syntax:

```
CREATE ROLE role_name;
```

Example:

```
CREATE ROLE data_analyst;
```

Granting Privileges to a Role:

Syntax:

```
GRANT privilege TO role_name;
```

Example:

```
GRANT SELECT, INSERT ON employees TO data_analyst;
```

Granting Roles to Users:

Syntax:

```
GRANT role_name TO username;
```

Example:

```
GRANT data_analyst TO john_doe;
```

Revoking Privileges and Roles:

Syntax:

```
REVOKE privilege ON object FROM username;
REVOKE role_name FROM username;
```

Example:

```
REVOKE SELECT ON employees FROM john_doe;
REVOKE data_analyst FROM john_doe;
```

9.3 Data Encryption

9.3.1 Introduction to Data Encryption

Data encryption protects sensitive data by converting it into an unreadable format, which can only be deciphered with the correct key. Oracle provides several encryption options to safeguard data.

9.3.2 Transparent Data Encryption (TDE)

TDE encrypts data at rest, ensuring that data files are encrypted on disk. TDE is configured at the tablespace or column level.

Enabling TDE:

1. **Create a Wallet**: The wallet stores encryption keys and must be configured before enabling TDE.

    Syntax:

    ```
    ADMINISTER KEY MANAGEMENT CREATE KEYSTORE
    'wallet_location' IDENTIFIED BY wallet_password;
    ```

    Example:

    ```
    ADMINISTER KEY MANAGEMENT CREATE KEYSTORE
    '/u01/app/oracle/admin/wallet' IDENTIFIED BY
    wallet_password;
    ```

2. **Open the Wallet**:

Syntax:

```
ADMINISTER KEY MANAGEMENT SET KEYSTORE OPEN
IDENTIFIED BY wallet_password;
```

Example:

```
ADMINISTER KEY MANAGEMENT SET KEYSTORE OPEN
IDENTIFIED BY wallet_password;
```

3. **Create an Encryption Key:**

    Syntax:

    ```
    ADMINISTER KEY MANAGEMENT SET ENCRYPTION KEY
    IDENTIFIED BY wallet_password;
    ```

    Example:

    ```
    ADMINISTER KEY MANAGEMENT SET ENCRYPTION KEY
    IDENTIFIED BY wallet_password;
    ```

4. **Encrypt a Tablespace:**

    Syntax:

    ```
    ALTER TABLESPACE tablespace_name ENCRYPTION
    ONLINE USING 'AES256';
    ```

    Example:

```
ALTER TABLESPACE users ENCRYPTION ONLINE USING
'AES256';
```

9.3.3 Column-Level Encryption

Column-level encryption allows for encrypting specific columns in a table, which is useful for protecting sensitive data such as Social Security numbers or credit card information.

Syntax:

```
CREATE TABLE employees (
    employee_id NUMBER,
    name VARCHAR2(50),
    ssn VARCHAR2(11) ENCRYPT USING 'AES256'
);
```

Example:

```
CREATE TABLE employees (
    employee_id NUMBER,
    name VARCHAR2(50),
    ssn VARCHAR2(11) ENCRYPT USING 'AES256'
);
```

9.4 Auditing

9.4.1 What is Auditing?

Auditing tracks and records database activities, such as login attempts, data modifications, and schema changes. Oracle provides a robust auditing framework to monitor and analyze database usage.

9.4.2 Enabling Auditing

1. **Basic Auditing**:

    Syntax:

    ```
    AUDIT statement ON object BY username;
    ```

    Example:

    ```
    AUDIT SELECT ON employees BY john_doe;
    ```

2. **Unified Auditing** (introduced in Oracle 12c):

    Unified auditing consolidates various auditing methods into a single framework, making it easier to manage and query audit data.

    Syntax:

    ```
    CREATE AUDIT POLICY policy_name ACTIONS ALL;
    ALTER SYSTEM SET audit_trail = 'DB,EXTENDED' SCOPE SPFILE;
    ```

Example:

```
CREATE AUDIT POLICY all_audit_policy ACTIONS ALL;
ALTER SYSTEM SET audit_trail = 'DB,EXTENDED' SCOPE SPFILE;
```

9.4.3 Reviewing Audit Logs

Syntax:

```
SELECT * FROM dba_audit_trail;
```

Example:

```
SELECT username, action_name, timestamp
FROM dba_audit_trail
WHERE username = 'john_doe';
```

9.5 Backup and Recovery

9.5.1 Backup Strategies

Regular backups are essential for data protection and recovery. Oracle provides several backup options, including:

1. **Full Backup**: A complete backup of the entire database.
2. **Incremental Backup**: Backs up only the changes made since the last backup.
3. **Cold Backup**: A backup taken while the database is offline.
4. **Hot Backup**: A backup taken while the database is online and operational.

9.5.2 Using RMAN for Backup and Recovery

Oracle Recovery Manager (RMAN) is a powerful tool for managing database backups and recovery.

Creating a Backup:

Syntax:

```
rman target /
BACKUP DATABASE;
```

Restoring a Backup:

Syntax:

```
rman target /
RESTORE DATABASE;
RECOVER DATABASE;
```

9.6 Conclusion

Database security is a multi-faceted discipline involving user management, privilege management, encryption, auditing, and backup strategies. In this chapter, we covered essential security features and practices in Oracle Database, including user management, roles and privileges, data encryption with TDE and column-level encryption, auditing, and backup and recovery strategies. By implementing these security measures, you can protect your data, maintain data integrity, and ensure compliance with regulatory requirements. In the next chapter, we will explore performance tuning and optimization techniques to enhance the efficiency of your Oracle Database operations.

Chapter 10: Performance Tuning and Optimization

Performance tuning and optimization are critical for ensuring that your Oracle Database operates efficiently and effectively. This chapter will cover techniques and strategies for enhancing database performance, including query optimization, indexing, and monitoring performance metrics.

10.1 Understanding Performance Tuning

10.1.1 What is Performance Tuning?

Performance tuning involves adjusting the database and application settings to improve the speed and efficiency of database operations. The goal is to minimize response times, reduce resource usage, and ensure smooth and reliable database performance.

10.1.2 Key Performance Metrics

1. **Response Time**: The time it takes for a query or operation to complete.
2. **Throughput**: The number of transactions or queries processed per unit of time.
3. **Resource Utilization**: The amount of CPU, memory, and I/O resources used by the database.

4. **Concurrency**: The ability of the database to handle multiple simultaneous operations without performance degradation.

10.2 Query Optimization

10.2.1 Analyzing and Improving Query Performance

Query performance can significantly impact overall database performance. Analyzing and optimizing queries involves examining execution plans, rewriting inefficient queries, and ensuring that queries are using appropriate indexes.

Using EXPLAIN PLAN:

The EXPLAIN PLAN statement provides insight into how the Oracle Database will execute a query, including the access paths and join methods used.

Syntax:

```
EXPLAIN PLAN FOR
SELECT * FROM employees WHERE department_id = 10;
```

Viewing the Execution Plan:

```
SELECT * FROM TABLE(DBMS_XPLAN.DISPLAY);
```

Example:

```
EXPLAIN PLAN FOR
SELECT * FROM employees WHERE department_id = 10;

SELECT * FROM TABLE(DBMS_XPLAN.DISPLAY);
```

Rewriting Inefficient Queries:

Consider rewriting queries to reduce complexity, avoid unnecessary joins, and use efficient filtering.

Example:

```
-- Inefficient query
SELECT * FROM employees WHERE department_id IN (10, 20, 30);

-- Optimized query
SELECT * FROM employees WHERE department_id = 10
UNION ALL
SELECT * FROM employees WHERE department_id = 20
UNION ALL
SELECT * FROM employees WHERE department_id = 30;
```

10.2.2 Using Indexes

Indexes can significantly improve query performance by reducing the amount of data that needs to be scanned.

Creating an Index:

Syntax:

```
CREATE INDEX index_name ON table_name (column_name);
```

Example:

```
CREATE INDEX idx_emp_dept ON employees (department_id);
```

Types of Indexes:

1. **B-Tree Indexes**: The default index type, suitable for most queries.
2. **Bitmap Indexes**: Useful for columns with low cardinality (few distinct values), such as gender.
3. **Function-Based Indexes**: Indexes based on expressions or functions, useful for queries involving computed values.

Example of a Bitmap Index:

```
CREATE BITMAP INDEX idx_emp_gender ON employees (gender);
```

Example of a Function-Based Index:

```
CREATE INDEX idx_emp_salary_dec ON employees (ROUND(salary, -3));
```

10.3 Index Management

10.3.1 Monitoring and Maintaining Indexes

Indexes require maintenance to ensure they remain efficient and effective.

Rebuilding Indexes:

Over time, indexes can become fragmented. Rebuilding an index can improve performance by reorganizing the index structure.

Syntax:

```
ALTER INDEX index_name REBUILD;
```

Example:

```
ALTER INDEX idx_emp_dept REBUILD;
```

Dropping Unused Indexes:

Indexes that are no longer used can be dropped to save space and reduce maintenance overhead.

Syntax:

```
DROP INDEX index_name;
```

Example:

```
DROP INDEX idx_old_index;
```

10.4 Performance Monitoring

10.4.1 Using Oracle Performance Views

Oracle provides several views for monitoring performance metrics and identifying potential issues.

V$SESSION: Provides information about active sessions and their activity.

Syntax:

```
SELECT * FROM V$SESSION WHERE STATUS = 'ACTIVE';
```

Example:

```
SELECT username, sid, serial#, status, machine
FROM V$SESSION
```

```
WHERE STATUS = 'ACTIVE';
```

V$SQL: Provides information about SQL statements currently in the shared pool.

Syntax:

```
SELECT sql_text, executions, elapsed_time
FROM V$SQL
ORDER BY elapsed_time DESC;
```

Example:

```
SELECT sql_text, executions, elapsed_time
FROM V$SQL
ORDER BY elapsed_time DESC;
```

V$SYSTEM_EVENT: Provides information about system-wide performance events.

Syntax:

```
SELECT event, total_waits, total_timeouts
FROM V$SYSTEM_EVENT;
```

Example:

```
SELECT event, total_waits, total_timeouts
FROM V$SYSTEM_EVENT;
```

10.4.2 Using Automatic Workload Repository (AWR)

AWR is a built-in performance monitoring and reporting tool in Oracle Database.

Generating an AWR Report:

1. **Run the AWR Report Generation**:

    Syntax:

    ```
    EXEC DBMS_WORKLOAD_REPOSITORY.CREATE_SNAPSHOT;
    ```

2. **Generate the Report**:

    Syntax:

    ```
    @?/rdbms/admin/awrrpt.sql
    ```

Example:

```
EXEC DBMS_WORKLOAD_REPOSITORY.CREATE_SNAPSHOT;
@?/rdbms/admin/awrrpt.sql
```

10.5 Database Tuning

10.5.1 Using the Oracle Tuning Advisor

The Oracle Tuning Advisor provides recommendations for improving SQL performance and optimizing database configurations.

Accessing the Tuning Advisor:

1. **Analyze SQL Statements:**

    Syntax:

    ```
    EXEC DBMS_SQLTUNE.CREATE_SQLSET('my_sqlset');
    EXEC DBMS_SQLTUNE.LOAD_SQLSET('my_sqlset', 'sql_id');
    EXEC DBMS_SQLTUNE.CREATE_TUNING_TASK('my_task', 'my_sqlset');
    ```

2. **View Recommendations:**

    Syntax:

    ```
    SELECT * FROM DBA_ADVISOR_RECOMMENDATIONS
    WHERE TASK_NAME = 'my_task';
    ```

Example:

```
EXEC DBMS_SQLTUNE.CREATE_SQLSET('my_sqlset');
EXEC DBMS_SQLTUNE.LOAD_SQLSET('my_sqlset', 'sql_id');
```

```sql
EXEC DBMS_SQLTUNE.CREATE_TUNING_TASK('my_task', 'my_sqlset');

SELECT * FROM DBA_ADVISOR_RECOMMENDATIONS WHERE TASK_NAME = 'my_task';
```

10.5.2 Configuring and Tuning the Oracle Instance

Memory Management:

Adjusting the memory settings can significantly impact performance. Key parameters include SGA_TARGET and PGA_AGGREGATE_TARGET.

Syntax:

```sql
ALTER SYSTEM SET SGA_TARGET = 2G;
ALTER SYSTEM SET PGA_AGGREGATE_TARGET = 1G;
```

Example:

```sql
ALTER SYSTEM SET SGA_TARGET = 2G;
ALTER SYSTEM SET PGA_AGGREGATE_TARGET = 1G;
```

Optimizing I/O Performance:

Ensure that database files are stored on high-performance storage systems and properly configured.

10.6 Best Practices for Performance Tuning

1. **Regularly Monitor Performance**: Use performance views and tools to continuously monitor database performance.
2. **Optimize Queries**: Rewrite inefficient queries and use indexes to improve query performance.
3. **Maintain Indexes**: Regularly rebuild and drop unused indexes to maintain efficiency.
4. **Use AWR Reports**: Generate and analyze AWR reports to identify performance bottlenecks and areas for improvement.
5. **Tune Database Configuration**: Adjust memory settings and optimize I/O performance based on workload requirements.

10.7 Conclusion

Performance tuning and optimization are essential for maintaining a high-performing Oracle Database. In this chapter, we explored techniques for optimizing queries, managing indexes, monitoring performance, and tuning the database instance. By applying these practices, you can enhance the efficiency of your database operations and ensure a smooth and responsive database environment. In the next chapter, we will explore advanced Oracle features and techniques to further extend your database capabilities.

Chapter 11: Advanced Oracle Features and Techniques

In this chapter, we will explore advanced features and techniques available in Oracle Database that can enhance your database capabilities and support complex business requirements. Topics include Oracle's partitioning and clustering features, advanced analytics, materialized views, and Oracle's spatial capabilities.

11.1 Oracle Partitioning

11.1.1 What is Partitioning?

Partitioning divides large tables or indexes into smaller, more manageable pieces called partitions. This improves performance and makes data management easier. Each partition can be managed and accessed independently.

11.1.2 Types of Partitioning

1. **Range Partitioning**: Divides data based on a range of values. Useful for data with a natural range, such as dates.

Syntax:

```
CREATE TABLE orders (
    order_id NUMBER,
    order_date DATE,
    amount NUMBER
)
PARTITION BY RANGE (order_date) (
    PARTITION p_2022 VALUES LESS THAN (TO_DATE('01-JAN-2023', 'DD-MON-YYYY')),
    PARTITION p_2023 VALUES LESS THAN (TO_DATE('01-JAN-2024', 'DD-MON-YYYY'))
);
```

Example:

```
CREATE TABLE orders (
    order_id NUMBER,
    order_date DATE,
    amount NUMBER
)
PARTITION BY RANGE (order_date) (
    PARTITION p_2022 VALUES LESS THAN (TO_DATE('01-JAN-2023', 'DD-MON-YYYY')),
    PARTITION p_2023 VALUES LESS THAN (TO_DATE('01-JAN-2024', 'DD-MON-YYYY'))
);
```

2. **List Partitioning**: Divides data based on discrete values. Useful for categorical data.

Syntax:

```
CREATE TABLE employees (
   emp_id NUMBER,
   department VARCHAR2(20)
)
PARTITION BY LIST (department) (
   PARTITION p_sales VALUES ('Sales'),
   PARTITION p_hr VALUES ('HR')
);
```

Example:

```
CREATE TABLE employees (
   emp_id NUMBER,
   department VARCHAR2(20)
)
PARTITION BY LIST (department) (
   PARTITION p_sales VALUES ('Sales'),
   PARTITION p_hr VALUES ('HR')
);
```

3. **Hash Partitioning**: Distributes data evenly across partitions using a hash function. Useful for load balancing.

Syntax:

```
CREATE TABLE transactions (
  txn_id NUMBER,
  txn_amount NUMBER
)
PARTITION BY HASH (txn_id) PARTITIONS 4;
```

Example:

```
CREATE TABLE transactions (
  txn_id NUMBER,
  txn_amount NUMBER
)
PARTITION BY HASH (txn_id) PARTITIONS 4;
```

4. **Composite Partitioning**: Combines multiple partitioning methods for more complex scenarios.

   Syntax:

```
CREATE TABLE sales (
  sale_id NUMBER,
  sale_date DATE,
  region VARCHAR2(20)
)
PARTITION BY RANGE (sale_date)
SUBPARTITION BY LIST (region)
(
```

```
    PARTITION p_2023 VALUES LESS THAN (TO_DATE('01-
JAN-2024', 'DD-MON-YYYY'))
  (
    SUBPARTITION sp_north VALUES ('North'),
    SUBPARTITION sp_south VALUES ('South')
  )
);
```

Example:

```
CREATE TABLE sales (
   sale_id NUMBER,
   sale_date DATE,
   region VARCHAR2(20)
)
PARTITION BY RANGE (sale_date)
SUBPARTITION BY LIST (region)
(
   PARTITION p_2023 VALUES LESS THAN (TO_DATE('01-
JAN-2024', 'DD-MON-YYYY'))
   (
     SUBPARTITION sp_north VALUES ('North'),
     SUBPARTITION sp_south VALUES ('South')
   )
);
```

11.2 Oracle Clustering

11.2.1 What is Clustering?

Clustering involves grouping related tables or indexes together to improve performance and manageability.

The Oracle Clusterware technology allows for high availability and scalability of database services.

11.2.2 Oracle Real Application Clusters (RAC)

Oracle RAC enables multiple instances to access a single database, providing high availability and load balancing.

Setting Up Oracle RAC:

1. **Install Oracle Grid Infrastructure**: Provides the foundation for clustering.
2. **Configure Cluster Nodes**: Set up multiple nodes to participate in the cluster.
3. **Create the RAC Database**: Use Oracle's Database Configuration Assistant (DBCA) to create a clustered database.

Example:

```
dbca -createDatabase -gdbName mydb -createAsCDB true -createAsCDB true -createPluggable true -createRAC true
```

11.3 Advanced Analytics

11.3.1 Oracle Analytics Features

Oracle provides several advanced analytics features to perform complex data analysis, including:

1. **Analytical SQL Functions**: Functions like RANK, DENSE_RANK, and NTILE for advanced querying.

   Syntax:

   ```
   SELECT employee_id, salary,
       RANK() OVER (ORDER BY salary DESC) AS salary_rank
   FROM employees;
   ```

   Example:

   ```
   SELECT employee_id, salary,
       RANK() OVER (ORDER BY salary DESC) AS salary_rank
   FROM employees;
   ```

2. **Oracle Data Mining**: Includes tools for predictive analytics, such as classification, regression, and clustering.

   Example:

   ```
   BEGIN
     DBMS_DATA_MINING.CREATE_MODEL(
       model_name => 'customer_churn_model',
       mining_function => DBMS_DATA_MINING.CLASSIFICATION,
       data_table_name => 'customer_data',
       case_id_column_name => 'customer_id',
       target_column_name => 'churn_flag'
     );
   END;
   ```

3. **Oracle OLAP**: Provides multidimensional analysis capabilities with OLAP cubes.

    Example:

    ```
    CREATE CUBE sales_cube
    DIMENSION BY (region, product, time)
    MEASURE sales_amount;
    ```

11.4 Materialized Views

11.4.1 What are Materialized Views?

Materialized views store the results of a query physically, allowing for faster query performance by precomputing and storing results.

11.4.2 Creating a Materialized View

Syntax:

```
CREATE MATERIALIZED VIEW mv_sales_summary
BUILD IMMEDIATE
REFRESH FAST ON COMMIT
AS
SELECT region, SUM(sales_amount) AS total_sales
FROM sales
GROUP BY region;
```

Example:

```
CREATE MATERIALIZED VIEW mv_sales_summary
BUILD IMMEDIATE
REFRESH FAST ON COMMIT
AS
SELECT region, SUM(sales_amount) AS total_sales
FROM sales
GROUP BY region;
```

11.4.3 Refreshing Materialized Views

Materialized views can be refreshed automatically or manually, depending on the refresh mode.

Syntax:

```
ALTER MATERIALIZED VIEW mv_sales_summary REFRESH;
```

Example:

```
ALTER MATERIALIZED VIEW mv_sales_summary REFRESH;
```

11.5 Oracle Spatial Capabilities

11.5.1 What is Oracle Spatial?

Oracle Spatial provides advanced capabilities for storing, querying, and analyzing spatial data, such as geographic locations and geometrical shapes.

11.5.2 Creating Spatial Tables

Syntax:

```
CREATE TABLE locations (
  id NUMBER,
  name VARCHAR2(100),
  location SDO_GEOMETRY
);
```

Example:

```
CREATE TABLE locations (
  id NUMBER,
  name VARCHAR2(100),
  location SDO_GEOMETRY
);
```

11.5.3 Using Spatial Queries

Spatial queries allow for querying spatial data using spatial functions.

Example:

```
SELECT name
FROM locations
WHERE SDO_NN(location, SDO_GEOMETRY(2001, 8307,
SDO_POINT_TYPE(1, 1, NULL), NULL, NULL), 'QUAD10') = 'TRUE';
```

11.6 Best Practices for Using Advanced Features

1. **Assess Business Needs**: Choose advanced features that align with your specific business requirements and use cases.
2. **Test Performance**: Before deploying advanced features, thoroughly test their impact on performance and resource usage.
3. **Monitor and Maintain**: Regularly monitor the performance and health of advanced features like partitioned tables and materialized views.
4. **Leverage Oracle Documentation**: Utilize Oracle's extensive documentation and resources to stay updated with the latest features and best practices.

11.7 Conclusion

Advanced Oracle features and techniques provide powerful tools to enhance database performance, manageability, and capabilities. In this chapter, we explored Oracle's partitioning and clustering features, advanced analytics, materialized views, and spatial capabilities. Understanding and effectively utilizing these features will help you build more robust and scalable database solutions. In the next chapter, we will explore Oracle's integration capabilities with other systems and technologies to extend the functionality of your database applications.

Chapter 12: Integrating Oracle with Other Systems and Technologies

Integration with other systems and technologies is essential for creating a cohesive IT environment and enabling data exchange across different platforms. In this chapter, we will explore various integration methods and technologies that work seamlessly with Oracle Database. Topics include Oracle's integration with web services, middleware, external data sources, and cloud platforms.

12.1 Integrating Oracle with Web Services

12.1.1 What are Web Services?

Web services allow different applications to communicate with each other over the web using standard protocols such as HTTP, XML, and SOAP. They enable interoperability between different systems regardless of their underlying technology.

12.1.2 Using Oracle XML DB for Web Services

Oracle XML DB provides native support for XML and web services. It includes features for publishing and consuming web services directly from the Oracle Database.

Creating a Web Service from a PL/SQL Procedure:

1. **Create a PL/SQL Procedure:**

   Syntax:

   ```
   CREATE OR REPLACE PROCEDURE get_employee_details (
     p_emp_id IN NUMBER,
     p_emp_name OUT VARCHAR2,
     p_emp_salary OUT NUMBER
   ) AS
   BEGIN
     SELECT employee_name, salary
     INTO p_emp_name, p_emp_salary
     FROM employees
     WHERE employee_id = p_emp_id;
   END;
   ```

   Example:

   ```
   CREATE OR REPLACE PROCEDURE get_employee_details (
     p_emp_id IN NUMBER,
     p_emp_name OUT VARCHAR2,
     p_emp_salary OUT NUMBER
   ) AS
   BEGIN
     SELECT employee_name, salary
     INTO p_emp_name, p_emp_salary
     FROM employees
     WHERE employee_id = p_emp_id;
   END;
   ```

2. **Publish the Procedure as a Web Service**:

   Syntax:

   ```
   BEGIN
     DBMS_HTTP.PUBLISH_WEB_SERVICE(
       web_service_name => 'get_employee_details',
       procedure_name => 'get_employee_details'
     );
   END;
   ```

   Example:

   ```
   BEGIN
     DBMS_HTTP.PUBLISH_WEB_SERVICE(
       web_service_name => 'get_employee_details',
       procedure_name => 'get_employee_details'
     );
   END;
   ```

12.1.3 Consuming Web Services in Oracle

Oracle can consume external web services using the UTL_HTTP package to send HTTP requests.

Syntax:

```
DECLARE
  l_response VARCHAR2(32767);
```

```
BEGIN
  l_response := UTL_HTTP.REQUEST('http://example.com/service');
  DBMS_OUTPUT.PUT_LINE(l_response);
END;
```

Example:

```
DECLARE
  l_response VARCHAR2(32767);
BEGIN
  l_response := UTL_HTTP.REQUEST('http://example.com/service');
  DBMS_OUTPUT.PUT_LINE(l_response);
END;
```

12.2 Middleware Integration

12.2.1 What is Middleware?

Middleware is software that acts as a bridge between different applications or systems, facilitating communication and data exchange. It can include Enterprise Service Bus (ESB), message queues, and integration platforms.

12.2.2 Oracle Fusion Middleware

Oracle Fusion Middleware provides a suite of tools for application integration, including:

1. **Oracle SOA Suite**: A comprehensive suite for building and deploying SOA (Service-Oriented Architecture) solutions.
2. **Oracle WebLogic Server**: An application server for running Java EE applications.
3. **Oracle Data Integrator (ODI)**: A tool for data integration and ETL (Extract, Transform, Load) processes.

Using Oracle SOA Suite:

1. **Create a Composite Application**:
   - Use Oracle JDeveloper to design composite applications that integrate various services and systems.
2. **Deploy the Application**:
   - Deploy the composite application to Oracle WebLogic Server.

Example:

- Design a composite application that integrates an external CRM system with an Oracle Database.

12.3 Integrating with External Data Sources

12.3.1 What are External Data Sources?

External data sources include other databases, file systems, and applications that provide data to be accessed or integrated with Oracle Database.

12.3.2 Using Database Links

Database links enable Oracle databases to connect and query data from other Oracle databases.

Creating a Database Link:

Syntax:

```
CREATE DATABASE LINK remote_db
CONNECT TO remote_user IDENTIFIED BY password
USING 'remote_db_tns';
```

Example:

```
CREATE DATABASE LINK remote_db
CONNECT TO remote_user IDENTIFIED BY password
USING 'remote_db_tns';
```

Querying Data Using a Database Link:

Syntax:

```
SELECT * FROM employees@remote_db;
```

Example:

```
SELECT * FROM employees@remote_db;
```

12.3.3 Using Oracle Heterogeneous Services

Oracle Heterogeneous Services allow Oracle databases to connect to non-Oracle data sources, such as SQL Server, DB2, or flat files.

Creating a Heterogeneous Service:

1. **Configure the ODBC Driver**: Install and configure the ODBC driver for the external data source.
2. **Create a Database Link**:

   Syntax:

   ```
   CREATE DATABASE LINK external_db
   CONNECT TO remote_user IDENTIFIED BY password
   USING 'external_service';
   ```

Example:

```
CREATE DATABASE LINK external_db
CONNECT TO remote_user IDENTIFIED BY password
USING 'external_service';
```

12.4 Cloud Integration

12.4.1 What is Cloud Integration?

Cloud integration involves connecting Oracle Database with cloud-based services and platforms. This enables scalability, flexibility, and access to cloud-based applications and data.

12.4.2 Oracle Cloud Services

1. **Oracle Autonomous Database**: A cloud service that automates database management tasks such as patching and tuning.
2. **Oracle Integration Cloud**: A cloud-based integration platform for connecting applications, data, and processes.

Integrating with Oracle Autonomous Database:

- Use Oracle Cloud Console to provision an Autonomous Database instance.

- Connect to the Autonomous Database using SQL Developer or other tools.

Example:

- Provision an Autonomous Database and migrate on-premises data to the cloud.

12.4.3 Using RESTful Services

Oracle Database supports RESTful web services for integrating with cloud applications and services.

Creating a RESTful Web Service:

1. **Create a RESTful Service Using Oracle REST Data Services (ORDS)**:

   Syntax:

   ```
   BEGIN
     ORDS.DEFINE_SERVICE(
       p_module_name   => 'employees',
       p_base_path     => '/employees/',
       p_items_per_page => 25,
       p_status        => 'PUBLISHED'
     );
   END;
   ```

Example:

```
BEGIN
  ORDS.DEFINE_SERVICE(
    p_module_name   => 'employees',
    p_base_path     => '/employees/',
    p_items_per_page => 25,
    p_status        => 'PUBLISHED'
  );
END;
```

2. **Access the RESTful Service**:
    - Use HTTP GET requests to access the data.

Example:

```
curl -X GET "http://example.com/ords/employees/"
```

12.5 Best Practices for Integration

1. **Ensure Security**: Implement appropriate security measures for data transfer and access control.
2. **Test Thoroughly**: Test integration points thoroughly to ensure reliability and performance.
3. **Monitor Integration**: Regularly monitor integration processes and troubleshoot issues as they arise.

4. **Document Integration Points**: Maintain clear documentation of integration points, configurations, and procedures.

12.6 Conclusion

Integrating Oracle Database with other systems and technologies enhances its capabilities and ensures a cohesive IT environment. In this chapter, we covered methods for integrating with web services, middleware, external data sources, and cloud platforms. By leveraging these integration techniques, you can build more flexible and robust database solutions that meet diverse business needs. In the next chapter, we will explore the principles of database security and strategies for protecting your Oracle Database environment.

Chapter 13: Database Security and Compliance

Ensuring the security and compliance of your Oracle Database is critical to protect sensitive data and meet regulatory requirements. This chapter will cover essential security practices, tools, and strategies for safeguarding your Oracle Database environment. Topics include user authentication and authorization, data encryption, auditing, and compliance with industry standards.

13.1 User Authentication and Authorization

13.1.1 Authentication

Authentication verifies the identity of users accessing the database. Oracle Database supports various authentication methods, including:

1. **Username/Password Authentication**: The most common method where users log in with a username and password.

Creating a User:

Syntax:

```
CREATE USER username IDENTIFIED BY password;
```

Example:

```
CREATE USER john_doe IDENTIFIED BY secure_password;
```

2. **Operating System Authentication**: Allows users to log in using their operating system credentials.

    Syntax:

    ```
    CREATE USER username IDENTIFIED EXTERNALLY;
    ```

    Example:

    ```
    CREATE USER os_user IDENTIFIED EXTERNALLY;
    ```

3. **LDAP Authentication**: Integrates with LDAP (Lightweight Directory Access Protocol) services for centralized authentication.

Example:

```
CREATE USER ldap_user IDENTIFIED BY ldap_password;
```

13.1.2 Authorization

Authorization determines what actions a user can perform within the database. It involves granting and revoking privileges.

1. **Granting Privileges**:

    Syntax:

    ```
    GRANT privilege TO user;
    ```

    Example:

    ```
    GRANT SELECT, INSERT ON employees TO john_doe;
    ```

2. **Revoking Privileges**:

    Syntax:

    ```
    REVOKE privilege FROM user;
    ```

Example:

```
REVOKE INSERT ON employees FROM john_doe;
```

3. **Roles**: Roles are collections of privileges that can be assigned to users.

   Creating a Role:

   Syntax:

   ```
   CREATE ROLE role_name;
   ```

   Example:

   ```
   CREATE ROLE data_analyst;
   ```

   Granting a Role:

   Syntax:

   ```
   GRANT role_name TO user;
   ```

   Example:

   ```
   GRANT data_analyst TO john_doe;
   ```

13.2 Data Encryption

13.2.1 Why Encrypt Data?

Data encryption protects sensitive information by converting it into an unreadable format that can only be decrypted with a key. This helps prevent unauthorized access to confidential data.

13.2.2 Transparent Data Encryption (TDE)

TDE provides encryption for data stored in the database. It encrypts data at the file level, ensuring that data is protected both at rest and in transit.

1. **Enabling TDE:**

    Syntax:

    ```
    CREATE TABLESPACE encrypted_tablespace
    ENCRYPTION USING 'AES256';
    ```

    Example:

    ```
    CREATE TABLESPACE encrypted_ts
    ENCRYPTION USING 'AES256';
    ```

2. **Encrypting Columns**:

   Syntax:

   ```
   CREATE TABLE secure_data (
     id NUMBER,
     sensitive_column VARCHAR2(100) ENCRYPT
   );
   ```

   Example:

   ```
   CREATE TABLE secure_data (
     id NUMBER,
     sensitive_column VARCHAR2(100) ENCRYPT
   );
   ```

13.2.3 Oracle Advanced Security

Oracle Advanced Security offers additional encryption features, such as:

1. **Column-Level Encryption**: Encrypts individual columns in a table.
2. **Data Redaction**: Masks sensitive data in query results to protect privacy.

Example:

```
BEGIN
  DBMS_REDACT.ADD_POLICY(
    object_schema => 'HR',
    object_name   => 'EMPLOYEES',
    column_name   => 'SALARY',
    policy_name   => 'salary_redaction',
    function_name => 'DBMS_REDACT.POLICY_NONE'
  );
END;
```

13.3 Auditing and Monitoring

13.3.1 Why Audit?

Auditing tracks database activities and changes, providing visibility into user actions and potential security incidents. It is essential for compliance and forensic analysis.

13.3.2 Configuring Auditing

1. **Basic Auditing**:

    Syntax:

    ```
    AUDIT SELECT ON employees BY ACCESS;
    ```

Example:

AUDIT SELECT ON employees BY ACCESS;

2. **Fine-Grained Auditing (FGA)**:

   FGA provides more granular auditing capabilities, allowing you to define policies for specific conditions.

   Syntax:

   ```
   BEGIN
     DBMS_FGA.ADD_POLICY(
       object_schema => 'HR',
       object_name   => 'EMPLOYEES',
       policy_name   => 'audit_salary_changes',
       audit_condition => 'SALARY > 100000'
     );
   END;
   ```

   Example:

   ```
   BEGIN
     DBMS_FGA.ADD_POLICY(
       object_schema => 'HR',
       object_name   => 'EMPLOYEES',
       policy_name   => 'audit_salary_changes',
       audit_condition => 'SALARY > 100000'
     );
   END;
   ```

13.3.3 Monitoring Tools

Oracle provides various tools for monitoring database performance and security, including:

1. **Oracle Enterprise Manager (OEM)**: A comprehensive tool for managing and monitoring Oracle databases.
2. **Automatic Workload Repository (AWR)**: Collects and reports on database performance metrics.
3. **Database Performance Analyzer (DPA)**: Provides insights into query performance and system health.

13.4 Compliance with Industry Standards

13.4.1 GDPR (General Data Protection Regulation)

GDPR requires organizations to protect personal data and provide data subjects with rights over their data.

Compliance Tips:

1. **Data Minimization**: Collect only the data necessary for your operations.
2. **User Consent**: Obtain explicit consent from users before collecting their data.
3. **Data Access Control**: Implement strict access controls and encryption for personal data.

13.4.2 HIPAA (Health Insurance Portability and Accountability Act)

HIPAA mandates the protection of health information and provides guidelines for securing electronic health records.

Compliance Tips:

1. **Encryption**: Encrypt sensitive health information both at rest and in transit.
2. **Audit Trails**: Maintain detailed audit trails for access to health information.
3. **Access Controls**: Implement role-based access controls and authentication mechanisms.

13.4.3 PCI-DSS (Payment Card Industry Data Security Standard)

PCI-DSS provides requirements for securing payment card information.

Compliance Tips:

1. **Data Encryption**: Encrypt payment card information both in transit and at rest.
2. **Regular Audits**: Conduct regular security audits and vulnerability assessments.
3. **Access Control**: Limit access to payment card information to authorized personnel only.

13.5 Best Practices for Database Security

1. **Regular Updates and Patching**: Keep your Oracle Database and its components updated with the latest security patches.
2. **Strong Authentication**: Use strong passwords, multi-factor authentication, and integrate with centralized authentication services.
3. **Data Encryption**: Implement encryption for sensitive data both at rest and in transit.
4. **Regular Audits**: Perform regular security audits and reviews to identify and address vulnerabilities.
5. **Access Controls**: Apply the principle of least privilege and use roles and privileges to control access to database resources.
6. **Backup and Recovery**: Ensure regular backups are taken and tested for recovery to protect against data loss.

13.6 Conclusion

Database security and compliance are crucial for protecting sensitive data and meeting regulatory requirements. In this chapter, we explored user authentication and authorization, data encryption, auditing, and compliance with industry standards. Implementing robust security practices and staying informed about compliance requirements will help ensure the integrity and confidentiality of your Oracle Database environment. In the next chapter, we will delve into best practices for database performance optimization and tuning to maximize the efficiency of your Oracle Database.

Chapter 14: Performance Optimization and Tuning

Database performance optimization is essential for ensuring that Oracle Database operates efficiently and can handle the demands of its users. This chapter explores key strategies and techniques for optimizing and tuning Oracle Database performance. We will cover database tuning fundamentals, query optimization, indexing, and monitoring tools.

14.1 Database Tuning Fundamentals

14.1.1 What is Database Tuning?

Database tuning involves adjusting database configurations, queries, and schema design to enhance performance and efficiency. Effective tuning ensures that the database can handle high loads, respond quickly to queries, and manage resources efficiently.

14.1.2 Key Performance Metrics

1. **Response Time**: The time taken for the database to respond to a query or request.
2. **Throughput**: The number of transactions or queries processed by the database per unit of time.

3. **Resource Utilization**: How efficiently the database uses CPU, memory, and disk resources.

14.2 Query Optimization

14.2.1 Understanding Query Execution Plans

The execution plan shows how Oracle Database executes a query. Analyzing execution plans helps identify performance bottlenecks.

Viewing Execution Plans:

Syntax:

```
EXPLAIN PLAN FOR <your_query>;
SELECT * FROM TABLE(DBMS_XPLAN.DISPLAY);
```

Example:

```
EXPLAIN PLAN FOR
SELECT * FROM employees WHERE department_id = 10;

SELECT * FROM TABLE(DBMS_XPLAN.DISPLAY);
```

14.2.2 SQL Query Optimization Techniques

1. **Use of Indexes**: Indexes improve query performance by allowing faster data retrieval.

Creating an Index:

Syntax:

```
CREATE INDEX index_name ON table_name
(column_name);
```

Example:

```
CREATE INDEX idx_dept_id ON employees
(department_id);
```

2. **Avoiding Full Table Scans**: Ensure queries use indexes rather than performing full table scans.
3. **Optimize Joins**: Use efficient join methods and avoid unnecessary joins.

Example:

```
SELECT e.employee_name, d.department_name
FROM employees e
JOIN departments d ON e.department_id =
d.department_id;
```

4. **Use Bind Variables**: Bind variables improve query performance and reduce parsing overhead.

Example:

```
SELECT * FROM employees WHERE department_id = :dept_id;
```

14.2.3 Reducing I/O Bottlenecks

1. **Optimize Disk Usage**: Ensure proper disk layout and distribution of data files.
2. **Use Oracle Automatic Storage Management (ASM)**: ASM simplifies storage management and improves performance.

Example:

```
ALTER DISKGROUP mydiskgroup ADD DISK '/dev/sdX';
```

14.3 Indexing Strategies

14.3.1 Types of Indexes

1. **B-Tree Indexes**: The default type of index that is suitable for most queries.
2. **Bitmap Indexes**: Useful for columns with low cardinality (few distinct values).

Creating a Bitmap Index:

Syntax:

```
CREATE BITMAP INDEX index_name ON table_name (column_name);
```

Example:

CREATE BITMAP INDEX idx_status ON employees (status);

3. **Function-Based Indexes:** Indexes on expressions or functions.

   Creating a Function-Based Index:

   Syntax:

   ```
   CREATE INDEX index_name ON table_name (function(column_name));
   ```

   Example:

   ```
   CREATE INDEX idx_lower_name ON employees (LOWER(employee_name));
   ```

14.3.2 Best Practices for Indexing

1. **Index Only What's Needed**: Avoid over-indexing, which can slow down DML operations (INSERT, UPDATE, DELETE).
2. **Monitor Index Usage**: Regularly check index usage and effectiveness.
3. **Rebuild Indexes**: Rebuild indexes periodically to optimize performance.

Syntax:

```
ALTER INDEX index_name REBUILD;
```

Example:

```
ALTER INDEX idx_dept_id REBUILD;
```

14.4 Monitoring and Diagnostics

14.4.1 Oracle Automatic Workload Repository (AWR)

AWR collects and stores performance statistics. It helps diagnose performance issues and identify areas for improvement.

1. **Generating AWR Reports**:

   Syntax:

   ```
   @?/rdbms/admin/awrrpt.sql
   ```

   Example:

   - Follow the prompts to generate an AWR report for a specified time range.

14.4.2 Oracle Enterprise Manager (OEM)

OEM provides a comprehensive graphical interface for monitoring and managing Oracle databases.

1. **Using OEM for Performance Monitoring**:
   - Navigate to the Performance tab in OEM to view real-time performance metrics and historical data.
   - Set up alerts and notifications for performance issues.

14.4.3 SQL Tuning Advisor

SQL Tuning Advisor provides recommendations for optimizing SQL queries.

1. **Running SQL Tuning Advisor**:

    Syntax:

    ```
    EXEC DBMS_SQLTUNE.CREATE_TUNING_TASK(
      sql_id => 'sql_id',
      task_name => 'tuning_task_name'
    );
    ```

    Example:

    ```
    EXEC DBMS_SQLTUNE.CREATE_TUNING_TASK(
      sql_id => 'abcd1234',
      task_name => 'tune_query'
    );
    ```

2. **Viewing Recommendations**:

    Syntax:

    ```
    EXEC DBMS_SQLTUNE.REPORT_TUNING_TASK('tuning_task_name');
    ```

    Example:

    ```
    EXEC DBMS_SQLTUNE.REPORT_TUNING_TASK('tune_query');
    ```

14.5 Best Practices for Performance Tuning

1. **Regularly Review Execution Plans**: Regularly check execution plans to ensure queries are optimized.
2. **Optimize Schema Design**: Properly design schema and relationships to minimize performance issues.
3. **Monitor Resource Utilization**: Continuously monitor CPU, memory, and I/O usage to prevent bottlenecks.
4. **Keep Statistics Up-to-Date**: Use DBMS_STATS to gather and maintain accurate statistics for the optimizer.

   Syntax:

   ```
   EXEC DBMS_STATS.GATHER_SCHEMA_STATS('schema_name');
   ```

   Example:

   ```
   EXEC DBMS_STATS.GATHER_SCHEMA_STATS('HR');
   ```

5. **Utilize Automatic Tuning Features**: Leverage Oracle's automatic tuning features like SQL Plan Management and Automatic SQL Tuning.

14.6 Conclusion

Performance optimization and tuning are crucial for maintaining an efficient and responsive Oracle Database. In this chapter, we covered database tuning fundamentals, query optimization techniques, indexing strategies, and monitoring tools. By applying these best practices and leveraging Oracle's performance features, you can ensure that your database performs optimally and meets the needs of its users. In the next chapter, we will explore advanced topics in Oracle Database management, including partitioning, clustering, and advanced recovery techniques.

Chapter 15: Advanced Oracle Database Management

As you become more proficient with Oracle Database, you may encounter advanced topics such as partitioning, clustering, and advanced recovery techniques. These features enhance database performance, scalability, and resilience. This chapter will cover these advanced management topics in detail.

15.1 Partitioning

15.1.1 What is Partitioning?

Partitioning divides a large table or index into smaller, more manageable pieces called partitions. Each partition can be stored separately, which can improve performance, manageability, and availability.

15.1.2 Types of Partitioning

1. **Range Partitioning**: Divides data based on a range of values. Useful for time-based data.

Example:

```
CREATE TABLE sales (
  sales_id NUMBER,
  sales_date DATE,
  amount NUMBER
)
PARTITION BY RANGE (sales_date) (
  PARTITION p_2022 VALUES LESS THAN (TO_DATE('01-JAN-2023', 'DD-MON-YYYY')),
  PARTITION p_2023 VALUES LESS THAN (TO_DATE('01-JAN-2024', 'DD-MON-YYYY'))
);
```

2. **List Partitioning**: Divides data based on a list of discrete values. Useful for categorical data.

   Example:

   ```
   CREATE TABLE employees (
     employee_id NUMBER,
     department_name VARCHAR2(50)
   )
   PARTITION BY LIST (department_name) (
     PARTITION p_sales VALUES ('Sales'),
     PARTITION p_hr VALUES ('HR')
   );
   ```

3. **Hash Partitioning**: Divides data based on a hash function. Useful for evenly distributing data.

Example:

```
CREATE TABLE orders (
  order_id NUMBER,
  order_date DATE
)
PARTITION BY HASH (order_id) PARTITIONS 4;
```

4. **Composite Partitioning**: Combines multiple partitioning methods.

Example:

```
CREATE TABLE transactions (
  transaction_id NUMBER,
  transaction_date DATE,
  region VARCHAR2(50)
)
PARTITION BY RANGE (transaction_date)
SUBPARTITION BY LIST (region) (
  PARTITION p_2023 VALUES LESS THAN (TO_DATE('01-JAN-2024', 'DD-MON-YYYY'))
    (SUBPARTITION sp_east VALUES ('East'),
     SUBPARTITION sp_west VALUES ('West'))
);
```

15.1.3 Benefits of Partitioning

1. **Improved Query Performance**: Queries can access only relevant partitions.

2. **Easier Data Management**: Manage partitions individually for maintenance and backups.
3. **Enhanced Availability**: Online operations can be performed on individual partitions.

15.2 Clustering

15.2.1 What is Clustering?

Clustering involves grouping related tables together to improve performance and manageability. The Oracle Real Application Clusters (RAC) is a key technology for clustering.

15.2.2 Oracle Real Application Clusters (RAC)

Oracle RAC allows multiple instances of Oracle Database to access the same database, providing high availability and scalability.

1. **Setting Up Oracle RAC**:
   - **Prerequisites**: Ensure that hardware and software requirements are met.
   - **Install Oracle Grid Infrastructure**: Provides the necessary infrastructure for RAC.

   Example:
   - Use the Oracle Universal Installer (OUI) to install and configure RAC.

2. **Configuring RAC**:
   - **Create a Database Cluster**: Use the Database Configuration Assistant (DBCA) to configure RAC.
   - **Manage RAC Instances**: Use Oracle Enterprise Manager or SQL*Plus to manage RAC instances.

15.2.3 Benefits of Oracle RAC

1. **High Availability**: Provides failover capabilities in case of instance or node failures.
2. **Scalability**: Allows the addition of new nodes to handle increased workload.
3. **Load Balancing**: Distributes workloads across multiple instances.

15.3 Advanced Recovery Techniques

15.3.1 What is Advanced Recovery?

Advanced recovery techniques involve methods for recovering data and databases beyond basic backup and restore operations. They are crucial for ensuring data integrity and availability in complex scenarios.

15.3.2 Flashback Technology

Flashback technology provides various features for recovering data to a previous state.

1. **Flashback Query**: Allows you to query data as it existed at a specific point in time.

   Example:

   ```
   SELECT * FROM employees AS OF TIMESTAMP
   (SYSTIMESTAMP - INTERVAL '1' DAY);
   ```

2. **Flashback Table**: Restores an entire table to a previous state.

   Syntax:

   ```
   FLASHBACK TABLE employees TO TIMESTAMP
   (SYSTIMESTAMP - INTERVAL '1' DAY);
   ```

   Example:

   ```
   FLASHBACK TABLE employees TO TIMESTAMP
   (SYSTIMESTAMP - INTERVAL '1' DAY);
   ```

3. **Flashback Database**: Restores the entire database to a previous point in time.

   Example:

   ```
   SHUTDOWN IMMEDIATE;
   STARTUP MOUNT;
   FLASHBACK DATABASE TO TIMESTAMP (SYSTIMESTAMP -
   INTERVAL '1' DAY);
   ALTER DATABASE OPEN RESETLOGS;
   ```

15.3.3 Oracle Data Guard

Oracle Data Guard provides disaster recovery and data protection by maintaining standby databases.

1. **Setting Up Data Guard**:
   - **Configure Primary and Standby Databases**: Use the Data Guard Broker or manual configuration methods.
   - **Manage Data Guard**: Use Oracle Data Guard Broker to manage the configuration.

   Example:
   - Use the Data Guard Broker to switch between primary and standby databases in case of failure.
2. **Benefits of Data Guard**:
   - **Disaster Recovery**: Provides a standby database that can be activated in case of primary database failure.
   - **Data Protection**: Ensures data is protected and synchronized across primary and standby databases.

15.4 Backup and Recovery Best Practices

1. **Regular Backups**: Perform regular backups using RMAN or other backup tools.

2. **Test Recovery Procedures**: Regularly test backup and recovery procedures to ensure they work as expected.
3. **Use Backup Redundancy**: Store backups in multiple locations to prevent data loss.
4. **Monitor Backup Jobs**: Monitor and manage backup jobs to ensure they complete successfully.

15.5 Conclusion

Advanced Oracle Database management techniques such as partitioning, clustering, and advanced recovery are essential for optimizing performance, ensuring high availability, and safeguarding data. In this chapter, we covered the benefits and implementation of these advanced features, helping you enhance your database environment. In the next chapter, we will explore database upgrade and migration strategies to ensure smooth transitions between different versions and platforms.

Chapter 16: Database Upgrade and Migration Strategies

Upgrading and migrating Oracle Databases are crucial for maintaining current software versions, leveraging new features, and ensuring compatibility with other systems. This chapter provides a comprehensive guide on how to plan and execute database upgrades and migrations effectively.

16.1 Understanding Database Upgrades

16.1.1 Why Upgrade?

Upgrading your Oracle Database can provide benefits such as:

1. **New Features**: Access to new functionalities and enhancements.
2. **Performance Improvements**: Better performance and optimization in the latest versions.
3. **Security Patches**: Protection against known vulnerabilities and threats.
4. **Compatibility**: Improved compatibility with other technologies and platforms.

16.1.2 Upgrade Methods

1. **Manual Upgrade**: Involves manually performing the upgrade steps using tools and commands.

    Steps:

    - Backup the existing database.
    - Install the new Oracle Database version.
    - Run the Database Upgrade Assistant (DBUA) or perform manual upgrade steps.

2. **Automated Upgrade**: Uses tools provided by Oracle to streamline the upgrade process.

    Tools:

    - **Database Upgrade Assistant (DBUA)**: A graphical tool for performing upgrades.
    - **Oracle Data Pump**: For exporting and importing data between versions.

    Example:

    ```
    dbua
    ```

3. **Rolling Upgrade**: Upgrades databases in a clustered environment without downtime.

Steps:

- Upgrade one node of the cluster at a time while others remain operational.
- Ensure that the upgrade process does not impact the cluster's availability.

16.2 Preparing for an Upgrade

16.2.1 Pre-Upgrade Checklist

1. **Review Compatibility**: Ensure that your application and hardware are compatible with the new version.
2. **Backup Data**: Perform a full backup of the existing database to prevent data loss.
3. **Check for Deprecated Features**: Identify and address features that are deprecated in the new version.
4. **Test the Upgrade**: Perform a test upgrade in a non-production environment to identify potential issues.

Example:

```
RMAN> BACKUP DATABASE;
```

16.2.2 Performing the Upgrade

1. **Using DBUA**:

- Start DBUA from the Oracle home directory.
- Follow the prompts to select the source and target databases, and configure upgrade options.

Example:

```
$ dbua
```

2. **Manual Upgrade**:
    - **Install New Oracle Version**: Install the new Oracle Database version on the target server.
    - **Run Pre-Upgrade Checks**: Use pre-upgrade checks to identify issues.

Syntax:

```
@?/preupgrade/preupgrade.sql TEXT
```

- **Perform the Upgrade**: Use the catctl.pl script to start the upgrade process.

Syntax:

```
$ perl $ORACLE_HOME/jdk/bin/java -jar $ORACLE_HOME/jdk/bin/catctl.jar
```

3. **Post-Upgrade Tasks**:
   - **Update Statistics**: Gather statistics for the upgraded database.

     Syntax:

     ```
     EXEC DBMS_STATS.GATHER_DATABASE_STATS;
     ```

   - **Validate the Upgrade**: Check database functionality and perform application testing.

16.3 Database Migration Strategies

16.3.1 What is Migration?

Database migration involves moving data from one database system or version to another. This could be due to changing platforms, consolidating databases, or transitioning to the cloud.

16.3.2 Migration Methods

1. **Data Pump**: Oracle Data Pump is a fast and efficient method for migrating data.

Exporting Data:

Syntax:

```
expdp username/password DIRECTORY=dp_dir
DUMPFILE=expdp_file.dmp LOGFILE=expdp_file.log
FULL=Y;
```

Importing Data:

Syntax:

```
impdp username/password DIRECTORY=dp_dir
DUMPFILE=expdp_file.dmp LOGFILE=impdp_file.log
FULL=Y;
```

2. **Transportable Tablespaces**: Moves entire tablespaces between databases.

    Steps:

    - **Prepare Tablespaces**: Make tablespaces read-only.

        Syntax:

        ```
        ALTER TABLESPACE tablespace_name READ ONLY;
        ```

    - **Export and Import**: Use Data Pump or traditional export/import methods.

3. **GoldenGate**: Oracle GoldenGate enables real-time data integration and migration.

   Steps:
   - **Install GoldenGate**: Install and configure GoldenGate on source and target systems.
   - **Configure Data Replication**: Set up data replication between databases.

4. **Manual Migration**: Involves exporting data using SQL scripts or other tools, then importing it into the new database.

   Steps:
   - **Export Data**: Use SQL scripts or other export methods.
   - **Import Data**: Load data into the target database.

16.4 Best Practices for Upgrade and Migration

1. **Plan Thoroughly**: Develop a detailed plan including timelines, resources, and potential risks.
2. **Perform Testing**: Conduct comprehensive testing in a staging environment before going live.

3. **Ensure Backup**: Always have a reliable backup before starting the upgrade or migration process.
4. **Monitor Performance**: After the upgrade or migration, monitor database performance to identify and address any issues.
5. **Communicate Changes**: Inform stakeholders about changes, timelines, and potential impacts.

16.5 Conclusion

Upgrading and migrating Oracle Databases require careful planning and execution to ensure a smooth transition. This chapter covered methods for upgrading and migrating databases, including preparation, execution, and best practices. By following these guidelines, you can successfully manage database upgrades and migrations, leveraging new features and maintaining database performance. In the next chapter, we will delve into database automation and scripting to further enhance your Oracle Database management capabilities.

Chapter 17: Database Automation and Scripting

Automation and scripting are crucial for managing Oracle Databases efficiently. They help streamline routine tasks, reduce human error, and improve overall database management. In this chapter, we will explore various methods for automating database operations and creating effective scripts to manage your Oracle Database.

17.1 Introduction to Database Automation

17.1.1 Why Automate?

Automating database tasks can lead to:

1. **Consistency**: Ensures that routine tasks are performed in a consistent manner.
2. **Efficiency**: Saves time and reduces the manual effort required for repetitive tasks.
3. **Error Reduction**: Minimizes the risk of human error in routine operations.

4. **Scalability**: Allows for handling larger environments with ease.

17.1.2 Key Automation Areas

1. **Backup and Recovery**: Automate backup schedules and recovery procedures.
2. **Monitoring and Alerts**: Set up automated monitoring and alerts for performance issues.
3. **Maintenance Tasks**: Schedule routine maintenance tasks such as gathering statistics or rebuilding indexes.

17.2 Oracle Scheduler

17.2.1 What is Oracle Scheduler?

Oracle Scheduler is a built-in feature of Oracle Database that allows you to automate and schedule database jobs and tasks.

17.2.2 Creating and Managing Jobs

1. **Creating a Job**:

   Syntax:

   ```
   BEGIN
     DBMS_SCHEDULER.CREATE_JOB (
        job_name       => 'job_name',
        job_type       => 'PLSQL_BLOCK',
        job_action     => 'BEGIN dbms_stats.gather_schema_stats; END;',
        start_date     => SYSTIMESTAMP,
        repeat_interval => 'FREQ=DAILY; BYHOUR=1',
        enabled        => TRUE
     );
   END;
   ```

   Example:

   ```
   BEGIN
     DBMS_SCHEDULER.CREATE_JOB (
        job_name       => 'daily_stats',
        job_type       => 'PLSQL_BLOCK',
        job_action     => 'BEGIN dbms_stats.gather_schema_stats; END;',
        start_date     => SYSTIMESTAMP,
        repeat_interval => 'FREQ=DAILY; BYHOUR=2',
        enabled        => TRUE
     );
   END;
   ```

2. **Viewing Job Status**:

    Syntax:

    ```
    SELECT job_name, status FROM dba_scheduler_jobs;
    ```

    Example:

    ```
    SELECT job_name, status FROM dba_scheduler_jobs;
    ```

3. **Managing Jobs**:
    - **Disable a Job**:

        Syntax:

        ```
        BEGIN
          DBMS_SCHEDULER.DISABLE('job_name');
        END;
        ```

        Example:

        ```
        BEGIN
          DBMS_SCHEDULER.DISABLE('daily_stats');
        END;
        ```

    - **Drop a Job**:

        Syntax:

        ```
        BEGIN
          DBMS_SCHEDULER.DROP_JOB('job_name');
        END;
        ```

Example:

```
BEGIN
  DBMS_SCHEDULER.DROP_JOB('daily_stats');
END;
```

17.3 SQL and PL/SQL Scripting

17.3.1 SQL Scripting

SQL scripts are used to automate tasks such as schema creation, data manipulation, and database administration.

1. **Writing SQL Scripts**:

    Example:

    ```
    -- Create a table
    CREATE TABLE employees (
      employee_id NUMBER PRIMARY KEY,
      employee_name VARCHAR2(100)
    );

    -- Insert data
    INSERT INTO employees (employee_id, employee_name)
    VALUES (1, 'John Doe');
    ```

2. **Running SQL Scripts**:
   - **Using SQL*Plus**:

   Syntax:

   ```
   sqlplus username/password @script.sql
   ```

   Example:

   ```
   sqlplus hr/hr_password @create_employees.sql
   ```

17.3.2 PL/SQL Scripting

PL/SQL is Oracle's procedural extension for SQL, allowing you to write complex scripts and programs.

1. **Writing PL/SQL Blocks**:

   Example:

   ```
   pl
   DECLARE
     v_employee_name VARCHAR2(100);
   BEGIN
     SELECT employee_name INTO v_employee_name
     FROM employees
     WHERE employee_id = 1;
     DBMS_OUTPUT.PUT_LINE('Employee Name: ' ||
   v_employee_name);
   END;
   ```

2. **Creating and Running PL/SQL Procedures:**
   - **Creating a Procedure:**

     Syntax:

     ```
     pl
     CREATE OR REPLACE PROCEDURE
     get_employee_name (p_emp_id IN NUMBER) AS
       v_employee_name VARCHAR2(100);
     BEGIN
       SELECT employee_name INTO v_employee_name
       FROM employees
       WHERE employee_id = p_emp_id;
       DBMS_OUTPUT.PUT_LINE('Employee Name: ' ||
     v_employee_name);
     END;
     ```

   - **Executing a Procedure:**

     Syntax:

     ```
     EXEC get_employee_name(1);
     ```

     Example:

     ```
     EXEC get_employee_name(1);
     ```

17.4 Automation Tools and Techniques

17.4.1 RMAN Scripts

Oracle RMAN (Recovery Manager) scripts automate backup and recovery operations.

1. **Creating RMAN Scripts**:

    Example:

    ```
    # Backup script
    RUN {
      ALLOCATE CHANNEL c1 DEVICE TYPE DISK;
      BACKUP DATABASE;
      RELEASE CHANNEL c1;
    }
    ```

2. **Running RMAN Scripts**:

    Syntax:

    ```
    rman target / @backup_script.rman
    ```

    Example:

    ```
    rman target / @backup_script.rman
    ```

17.4.2 Oracle Enterprise Manager (OEM) Automation

OEM provides a graphical interface for automating and managing database tasks.

1. **Creating and Scheduling Jobs in OEM:**
   - **Navigate to Jobs**: Go to the Jobs section in Oracle Enterprise Manager.
   - **Create a New Job**: Define the job type, schedule, and actions.
   - **Monitor Job Execution**: Track job status and review logs.
2. **Using OEM for Performance Monitoring**:
   - **Set Up Alerts**: Configure alerts for performance thresholds.
   - **View Performance Metrics**: Use OEM dashboards to monitor real-time performance.

17.5 Best Practices for Scripting and Automation

1. **Modularize Scripts**: Break down complex tasks into smaller, reusable scripts.
2. **Test Thoroughly**: Test scripts in a development or staging environment before deploying them in production.

3. **Document Scripts**: Provide clear comments and documentation within scripts to explain their purpose and usage.
4. **Implement Error Handling**: Include error handling in scripts to manage exceptions and ensure smooth execution.
5. **Monitor and Audit**: Regularly review and audit automated tasks to ensure they are performing as expected.

17.6 Conclusion

Database automation and scripting are essential for efficient Oracle Database management. By leveraging tools such as Oracle Scheduler, SQL/PL/SQL scripting, and automation tools, you can streamline routine tasks, enhance consistency, and improve overall database operations. This chapter has provided insights into automation strategies and scripting techniques to help you manage your Oracle Database effectively. In the next chapter, we will explore database security best practices to ensure the safety and integrity of your data.

Chapter 18: Database Security Best Practices

Ensuring the security of your Oracle Database is crucial for protecting sensitive data and maintaining compliance with regulations. This chapter will explore best practices for database security, including user management, access control, encryption, and auditing.

18.1 Introduction to Database Security

18.1.1 Why Database Security is Important

Database security is essential for:

1. **Protecting Data**: Safeguards sensitive and critical information from unauthorized access and breaches.
2. **Maintaining Compliance**: Ensures adherence to regulatory requirements such as GDPR, HIPAA, and PCI-DSS.
3. **Preventing Data Loss**: Mitigates risks of data loss due to malicious activities or accidental actions.
4. **Maintaining Integrity**: Ensures the accuracy and reliability of data.

18.2 User Management and Access Control

18.2.1 User Accounts and Roles

1. **Creating User Accounts**:

    Syntax:

    ```
    CREATE USER username IDENTIFIED BY password;
    ```

    Example:

    ```
    CREATE USER john_doe IDENTIFIED BY securePass123;
    ```

2. **Granting Roles and Privileges**:
    - **Granting Roles**:

        Syntax:

        ```
        GRANT role_name TO username;
        ```

        Example:

        ```
        GRANT DBA TO john_doe;
        ```

    - **Granting Privileges**:

        Syntax:

        ```
        GRANT privilege ON object TO username;
        ```

Example:

```
GRANT SELECT ON employees TO john_doe;
```

3. **Creating Roles**:

   Syntax:

   ```
   CREATE ROLE role_name;
   ```

   Example:

   ```
   CREATE ROLE data_analyst;
   ```

   Granting Privileges to Roles:

   Syntax:

   ```
   GRANT SELECT, INSERT ON employees TO data_analyst;
   ```

   Example:

   ```
   GRANT SELECT, INSERT ON employees TO data_analyst;
   ```

18.2.2 Managing User Sessions

1. **Viewing User Sessions**:

   Syntax:

   ```
   SELECT * FROM v$session WHERE username = 'username';
   ```

Example:

```
SELECT * FROM v$session WHERE username = 'john_doe';
```

2. **Terminating User Sessions**:

   Syntax:

   ```
   ALTER SYSTEM KILL SESSION 'sid,serial#';
   ```

   Example:

   ```
   ALTER SYSTEM KILL SESSION '123,4567';
   ```

18.3 Encryption

18.3.1 Data Encryption Techniques

1. **Transparent Data Encryption (TDE)**:

   TDE provides encryption for data at rest.

   Creating a Wallet:

   Syntax:

   ```
   ADMINISTER KEY MANAGEMENT CREATE KEYSTORE
   'path_to_wallet' IDENTIFIED BY password;
   ```

Example:

```
ADMINISTER KEY MANAGEMENT CREATE KEYSTORE
'/u01/app/oracle/wallet' IDENTIFIED BY myWalletPass;
```

Enabling TDE:

Syntax:

```
ALTER SYSTEM SET ENCRYPTION KEY IDENTIFIED BY
password;
```

Example:

```
ALTER SYSTEM SET ENCRYPTION KEY IDENTIFIED BY
myWalletPass;
```

Encrypting Tablespaces:

Syntax:

```
ALTER TABLESPACE tablespace_name ENCRYPTION
ONLINE USING 'AES256' ENCRYPT;
```

Example:

```
ALTER TABLESPACE users ENCRYPTION ONLINE USING
'AES256' ENCRYPT;
```

2. **Column-Level Encryption**:

   Syntax:

   ```
   CREATE TABLE sensitive_data (
     id NUMBER,
     sensitive_column VARCHAR2(100) ENCRYPT USING 'AES256'
   );
   ```

   Example:

   ```
   CREATE TABLE sensitive_data (
     id NUMBER,
     sensitive_column VARCHAR2(100) ENCRYPT USING 'AES256'
   );
   ```

18.3.2 Network Encryption

Network encryption protects data transmitted between the client and server.

1. **Configuring Oracle Net Services Encryption**:

   Steps:
   - Edit the sqlnet.ora configuration file.
   - Specify encryption and integrity algorithms.

Example Configuration:

```
SQLNET.ENCRYPTION_TYPES_SERVER = (AES256)
SQLNET.ENCRYPTION_TYPES_CLIENT = (AES256)
SQLNET.CRYPTO_CHECKSUM_TYPES_SERVER = (SHA256)
SQLNET.CRYPTO_CHECKSUM_TYPES_CLIENT = (SHA256)
```

18.4 Auditing

18.4.1 What is Auditing?

Auditing tracks and records database activities to monitor and review user actions and detect potential security issues.

18.4.2 Configuring Auditing

1. **Enabling Auditing**:

   Syntax:

   ```
   AUDIT ALL BY username BY ACCESS;
   ```

   Example:

   ```
   AUDIT SELECT ON employees BY ACCESS;
   ```

2. **Viewing Audit Logs**:

   Syntax:

   ```
   SELECT * FROM dba_audit_trail;
   ```

   Example:

   ```
   SELECT * FROM dba_audit_trail;
   ```

3. **Managing Audit Trails**:
   - **Purging Old Audit Records**:

     Syntax:

     ```
     BEGIN
       DBMS_AUDIT_MGMT.CLEAN_AUDIT_TRAIL(
         audit_trail_type =>
     DBMS_AUDIT_MGMT.AUDIT_TRAIL_ALL,
         retention_period => 30
       );
     END;
     ```

     Example:

     ```
     BEGIN
       DBMS_AUDIT_MGMT.CLEAN_AUDIT_TRAIL(
         audit_trail_type =>
     DBMS_AUDIT_MGMT.AUDIT_TRAIL_ALL,
         retention_period => 30
       );
     END;
     ```

18.5 Best Practices for Database Security

1. **Apply the Principle of Least Privilege**: Grant only the necessary permissions to users and roles.
2. **Regularly Update and Patch**: Keep your database software updated with the latest patches and security fixes.
3. **Encrypt Sensitive Data**: Use encryption to protect data at rest and in transit.
4. **Monitor and Audit**: Continuously monitor database activities and review audit logs for suspicious activities.
5. **Backup and Recover**: Implement a robust backup and recovery strategy to protect data from loss or corruption.
6. **Secure Network Connections**: Use secure protocols and encryption for network communication between clients and the database.

18.6 Conclusion

Database security is critical for protecting sensitive information and maintaining regulatory compliance. This chapter has covered key security practices, including user management, encryption, and auditing, to help you secure your Oracle Database environment. By implementing these best practices, you can enhance the security and integrity of your database and safeguard against potential threats. In the next chapter, we will explore performance tuning and optimization techniques to ensure your Oracle Database operates efficiently.

Chapter 19: Performance Tuning and Optimization

Optimizing database performance is essential for ensuring that your Oracle Database operates efficiently and meets the needs of your users and applications. This chapter will cover key strategies for performance tuning and optimization, including monitoring, indexing, query optimization, and configuration adjustments.

19.1 Introduction to Performance Tuning

19.1.1 Why Performance Tuning is Important

Performance tuning is crucial because:

1. **Improves Response Time**: Reduces the time it takes for queries to execute and return results.
2. **Enhances User Experience**: Ensures that applications and users experience minimal delays and high availability.
3. **Optimizes Resource Usage**: Efficient use of CPU, memory, and I/O resources.
4. **Reduces Costs**: Minimizes hardware and software costs associated with poor performance.

19.2 Monitoring Database Performance

19.2.1 Key Performance Metrics

1. **CPU Usage**: Measures the amount of CPU resources consumed by the database.
2. **Memory Usage**: Monitors the memory allocated and used by the database processes.
3. **Disk I/O**: Tracks read and write operations on the disk.
4. **Query Response Time**: Measures the time taken to execute queries.

19.2.2 Using Oracle Performance Monitoring Tools

1. **Oracle Enterprise Manager (OEM)**:
    - **Overview**: Provides a graphical interface for monitoring and managing database performance.
    - **Key Features**: Real-time performance dashboards, alerting, and diagnostic tools.

    Example:

    - Access OEM via the web interface and navigate to the Performance tab to view real-time metrics.
2. **Automatic Workload Repository (AWR)**:

- **Overview**: Collects and reports performance data over time.
- **Generating AWR Reports**:

  Syntax:

  ```
  EXEC DBMS_WORKLOAD_REPOSITORY.CREATE_REPCRT (
    report_type => 'HTML',
    report_format => 'HTML',
    report_interval => '1 DAY'
  );
  ```

  Example:

  ```
  EXEC DBMS_WORKLOAD_REPOSITORY.CREATE_REPCRT (
    report_type => 'HTML',
    report_format => 'HTML',
    report_interval => '1 DAY'
  );
  ```

3. **Statspack**:
   - **Overview**: Provides performance metrics similar to AWR but is available in earlier Oracle versions.
   - **Generating Statspack Reports**:

Syntax:

```
@?/stats/admin/spreport.sql
```

Example:

```
@?/stats/admin/spreport.sql
```

19.3 Query Optimization

19.3.1 Understanding Query Execution Plans

1. **What is an Execution Plan?**

   An execution plan outlines how the Oracle Database will execute a SQL query, including the steps and resources required.

2. **Viewing Execution Plans:**

   Syntax:

   ```
   EXPLAIN PLAN FOR query;
   SELECT * FROM table(DBMS_XPLAN.DISPLAY);
   ```

Example:

```
EXPLAIN PLAN FOR
SELECT * FROM employees WHERE employee_id = 1;
SELECT * FROM table(DBMS_XPLAN.DISPLAY);
```

19.3.2 Indexing Strategies

1. **Creating Indexes**:

   Syntax:

   ```
   CREATE INDEX index_name ON
   table_name(column_name);
   ```

   Example:

   ```
   CREATE INDEX idx_employee_id ON
   employees(employee_id);
   ```

2. **Types of Indexes**:
   - **B-Tree Indexes**: Default index type for general use.
   - **Bitmap Indexes**: Efficient for columns with a low number of distinct values.
   - **Function-Based Indexes**: Indexes based on expressions or functions.

Example:

```
CREATE INDEX idx_lower_name ON
employees(LOWER(employee_name));
```

3. **Index Maintenance**:
   - **Rebuilding Indexes**:

     Syntax:

     ```
     ALTER INDEX index_name REBUILD;
     ```

     Example:

     ```
     ALTER INDEX idx_employee_id REBUILD;
     ```

   - **Monitoring Index Usage**:

     Syntax:

     ```
     SELECT * FROM dba_indexes WHERE index_name = 'index_name';
     ```

     Example:

     ```
     SELECT * FROM dba_indexes WHERE index_name = 'idx_employee_id';
     ```

19.4 Optimizing Database Configuration

19.4.1 Memory Configuration

1. **Sizing SGA and PGA**:
   - **System Global Area (SGA)**: Shared memory area used by Oracle processes.
   - **Program Global Area (PGA)**: Memory area used by a single Oracle process.

   Syntax:

   ```
   ALTER SYSTEM SET SGA_TARGET = size;
   ALTER SYSTEM SET PGA_AGGREGATE_TARGET = size;
   ```

   Example:

   ```
   ALTER SYSTEM SET SGA_TARGET = 2G;
   ALTER SYSTEM SET PGA_AGGREGATE_TARGET = 1G;
   ```

2. **Using Automatic Memory Management (AMM)**:

   Syntax:

   ```
   ALTER SYSTEM SET MEMORY_TARGET = size;
   ```

Example:

```
ALTER SYSTEM SET MEMORY_TARGET = 3G;
```

19.4.2 Optimizing Disk I/O

1. **Using Oracle Automatic Storage Management (ASM)**:
   - **Overview**: Provides a high-performance storage management solution.

   Example:

   - Configure ASM using the asmca utility.

2. **Configuring Redo Logs and Data Files**:

   Syntax:

   ```
   ALTER DATABASE ADD LOGFILE ('path_to_logfile');
   ALTER DATABASE DATAFILE 'path_to_datafile' RESIZE size;
   ```

   Example:

   ```
   ALTER DATABASE ADD LOGFILE ('/u01/app/oracle/oradata/redo01.log');
   ALTER DATABASE DATAFILE '/u01/app/oracle/oradata/system01.dbf' RESIZE 2G;
   ```

19.5 Monitoring and Managing Performance

19.5.1 Identifying Performance Bottlenecks

1. **Using AWR Reports**: Analyze AWR reports to identify performance issues and trends.
2. **SQL Tuning**: Use tools such as Oracle SQL Tuning Advisor to recommend optimizations.

Syntax:

```
EXEC DBMS_SQLTUNE.CREATE_TUNING_TASK (
  sql_id => 'sql_id',
  task_name => 'task_name'
);
EXEC DBMS_SQLTUNE.EXECUTE_TUNING_TASK ('task_name');
```

Example:

```
EXEC DBMS_SQLTUNE.CREATE_TUNING_TASK (
  sql_id => '4j2q4y0s08h7z',
  task_name => 'tune_task'
);
EXEC DBMS_SQLTUNE.EXECUTE_TUNING_TASK ('tune_task');
```

19.5.2 Adjusting Database Parameters

1. **Dynamic Parameters**: Modify parameters that can be changed without restarting the database.

   Syntax:

   ```
   ALTER SYSTEM SET parameter_name = value;
   ```

   Example:

   ```
   ALTER SYSTEM SET optimizer_mode = 'ALL_ROWS';
   ```

2. **Static Parameters**: Modify parameters that require a database restart.

   Example:

   - Edit the init.ora or spfile.ora configuration file and restart the database.

19.6 Best Practices for Performance Tuning

1. **Regularly Monitor Performance**: Continuously monitor performance metrics to proactively address issues.
2. **Optimize Queries**: Use execution plans and indexing strategies to enhance query performance.

3. **Adjust Configuration Settings**: Fine-tune memory and I/O settings based on workload requirements.
4. **Test Changes in Staging**: Test performance tuning changes in a staging environment before applying them to production.
5. **Document and Review**: Document performance tuning efforts and review them periodically to ensure ongoing optimization.

19.7 Conclusion

Performance tuning and optimization are key to maintaining a responsive and efficient Oracle Database environment. This chapter has covered various aspects of performance tuning, including monitoring, query optimization, indexing, and configuration adjustments. By implementing these practices, you can ensure that your Oracle Database operates at its best, providing a seamless experience for users and applications. In the next chapter, we will explore advanced topics such as data warehousing and analytics to further enhance your database capabilities.

Chapter 20: Data Warehousing and Analytics

Data warehousing and analytics are crucial for organizations that need to analyze large volumes of data to gain business insights and support decision-making. This chapter will explore the fundamentals of data warehousing, the role of Oracle in data warehousing solutions, and how to leverage analytics tools to extract meaningful information from your data.

20.1 Introduction to Data Warehousing

20.1.1 What is a Data Warehouse?

A data warehouse is a centralized repository that allows you to store and analyze large volumes of structured data from multiple sources. It supports business intelligence (BI) activities, including data analysis, reporting, and data mining.

20.1.2 Key Characteristics of Data Warehouses

1. **Subject-Oriented**: Organized around key business subjects (e.g., sales, finance).
2. **Integrated**: Combines data from various sources into a coherent structure.
3. **Non-Volatile**: Data is stable and not subject to frequent changes.

4. **Time-Variant**: Historical data is retained for analysis over time.

20.2 Oracle Data Warehousing Solutions

20.2.1 Oracle Exadata

1. **Overview**: Oracle Exadata is a high-performance data warehousing appliance that combines hardware and software optimized for database workloads.
2. **Key Features**:
   - **High Performance**: Engineered for fast query performance and high availability.
   - **Scalability**: Easily scalable to handle increasing data volumes.
   - **Integrated Storage and Compute**: Optimized for both transactional and analytical processing.

20.2.2 Oracle Autonomous Data Warehouse

1. **Overview**: A cloud-based data warehousing service that automates database management tasks such as provisioning, tuning, and patching.
2. **Key Features**:
   - **Self-Driving**: Automated tuning, patching, and upgrades.
   - **Scalable**: Elastic scalability to handle varying workloads.

- **Secure**: Built-in security features to protect data.

20.3 Designing a Data Warehouse

20.3.1 Data Warehouse Architecture

1. **Data Sources**: Systems and databases that provide data to the warehouse (e.g., ERP systems, CRM systems).
2. **ETL Process**: Extract, Transform, Load (ETL) processes to move data from sources to the warehouse.
3. **Data Warehouse**: The central repository where data is stored and organized.
4. **BI Tools**: Tools for querying and analyzing data (e.g., Oracle Analytics Cloud).

20.3.2 Data Modeling

1. **Star Schema**: A type of schema where a central fact table is connected to dimension tables.

    Example:

    - **Fact Table**: Sales (with columns for sales amount, date, product ID, etc.)
    - **Dimension Tables**: Date, Product, Customer

2. **Snowflake Schema**: A normalized version of the star schema where dimension tables are further divided into sub-dimensions.

   Example:

   - **Fact Table**: Sales
   - **Dimension Tables**: Date, Product (with sub-dimensions for Product Category and Product Brand)

20.4 Querying and Analyzing Data

20.4.1 Using SQL for Data Analysis

1. **Basic SQL Queries**:

   Example:

   ```
   SELECT product_name, SUM(sales_amount) AS total_sales
   FROM sales
   GROUP BY product_name
   ORDER BY total_sales DESC;
   ```

2. **Complex SQL Queries**:

   Example:

   ```
   SELECT
     c.customer_name,
     p.product_name,
     SUM(s.sales_amount) AS total_sales
   ```

```
FROM sales s
JOIN customers c ON s.customer_id = c.customer_id
JOIN products p ON s.product_id = p.product_id
WHERE s.sales_date BETWEEN TO_DATE('2023-01-01',
'YYYY-MM-DD') AND TO_DATE('2023-12-31', 'YYYY-MM-
DD')
GROUP BY c.customer_name, p.product_name
ORDER BY total_sales DESC;
```

20.4.2 Using Oracle Analytics Cloud

1. **Overview**: Oracle Analytics Cloud (OAC) provides advanced analytics and visualization tools.
2. **Creating Dashboards**:
   - **Connecting to Data Sources**: Import data from Oracle Database or other sources.
   - **Building Reports**: Create interactive reports and visualizations.
   - **Exploring Data**: Use features like data discovery and predictive analytics to gain insights.

Example:

- Create a sales dashboard to visualize key metrics such as total sales, sales by region, and top-performing products.

20.5 Data Warehousing Best Practices

1. **Define Clear Objectives**: Establish clear goals for your data warehouse to guide design and implementation.
2. **Ensure Data Quality**: Implement data cleansing and validation processes to ensure accurate and reliable data.
3. **Optimize ETL Processes**: Efficiently design ETL processes to handle large data volumes and minimize load times.
4. **Implement Security Measures**: Protect data with encryption, access controls, and regular audits.
5. **Regularly Monitor Performance**: Continuously monitor the performance of your data warehouse and optimize as needed.

20.6 Conclusion

Data warehousing and analytics are powerful tools for organizations seeking to leverage their data for strategic decision-making. This chapter has covered the fundamentals of data warehousing, Oracle's data warehousing solutions, data modeling, and analytics techniques. By implementing these practices and tools, you can build a robust data warehousing environment that provides valuable insights and supports business intelligence initiatives. In the next chapter, we will explore advanced Oracle features and integrations to further enhance your database capabilities.